Tom Wilmer had me at the title. *Romancing the Coast: Romantic Getaways Along the California Coast*—it's exactly where I want to be and exactly what I want to be doing. You couldn't ask for a better travel companion than this many-miled writer. Here are carefully chosen best stays along the best coast. All you have to do is choose the particular paradise that suits your personal idea of romantic bliss.

DANA JOSEPH
Cowboys and Indians Magazine

Filled with personal observations and valuable tips, this is the best collection of California coastal hideaways I've seen. Makes me want to rent a ragtop, bring a special friend, and hit every place Tom Wilmer has recommended. And I just may do it!

BOB KAPPSTATTER
New York Daily News

Romancing the Coast

Romancing the Coast

Romantic Getaways Along the California Coast

By Thomas C. Wilmer

RiverWood Books
Ashland, Oregon

Cover by David Ruppe, Impact Publications
Interior by Christy Collins

Printed in the United States

Library of Congress Cataloging-in-Publication Data

Wilmer, Thomas C., 1949-
Romancing the coast : romantic getaways along the California coast / by Thomas
C. Wilmer.
p. cm.
ISBN 1-883991-80-3 (pbk.)
1. Hotels--California--Pacific Coast--Guidebook. 2. Resorts--California--Pacific
Coast--Guidebooks. I. Title.
TX907.3.P33W57 2004
917.9506'144--dc22
2004000650

DEDICATION

To the memory of my father

Heartfelt thanks to my mom; brothers John, Jim, and sister Mary; wife Beth; daughters Celena, Merissa, and Mary; in-laws Gene and Ginnie, Gabe, Howard, and John.

It is amazing how many people—friends and family, fellow journalists, and travelers met on the road—have extended support, encouragement, and invaluable insights while researching and writing this book. I am especially indebted to the contributing writer/field researchers who supplied so much in so many ways, from independently inspecting various properties to providing last-minute updates and fresh insights about the inns and resorts. Without the invaluable assistance of contributors Marian Jane Sanders, Leslie Westbrook, Richard Torregrossa, Marissa Waddell, Ginny Craven, and Stephen Scholl at White Cloud Press, me thinks I'd still be madly driving up and down the state, inspecting and re-inspecting inns and resorts—ad infinitum.

An indebted thanks to: John King and his assistant Mimi Lyon, Gus and Debbie Nelson, Timothy Conn, Thor and Julie Conway, the staff at NPR affiliate KCBX, Brent Smith, Steve Weeks, lifelong friend Rory McDonald, and especially his late father George (who ardently encouraged me along the way), Bill Tomicki, Professor James Fetler, Shirley and John Ledgerwood, Steve Moss, Mark Wimberly, Hollis, Michael and Ann Vidor, Annie and Judge James Ream, Stephen McGrath, Father Tony Grinell, Tony Donelly in Northern Ireland, Marilyn Bauer, Dave and Tanja Worthely, and Queenie.

NORTH COAST

• Eureka

• Mendocino

SAN FRANCISCO BAY

• Napa/Sonoma
• Sausalito
• San Francisco

SANTA CRUZ

MONTEREY PENINSULA • Carmel

BIG SUR

• San Luis Obispo

CENTRAL COAST

• Santa Barbara

• Los Angeles

• Laguna Beach

CATALINA ISLAND

SOUTHERN CALIFORNIA

La Jolla
• San Diego

Table of Contents

Paradise Found

by Thomas C. Wilmer

The intent of *Romancing the Coast* is to offer you an insider's in-depth look at coastal California's truly world-class resorts, inns, hotels, and B&Bs. If you're seeking pure unadulterated romance and savory memories, then read on.

California's coastline is enormously long—approximately ten degrees of latitude. To explore the equivalent coastal section in Europe, one would begin the journey around Casablanca, Morocco (San Diego), cross the Straits of Gibraltar, travel along the shores of Spain's Gulf of Cadiz and the length of Portugal before completing the quest around Lisbon (the Oregon border)

California's coastal region offers the traveler a spectacularly diverse array of experiences. In the north, you feel the majesty of 2,000 year-old behemoth redwoods, and in the land of Big Sur you stand awestruck in the precipitous coastal mountains that thrust nearly straight up from the sea, 3,000 feet and more. Big Sur country stops abruptly around San Simeon (the home of Hearst Castle). Continuing southbound, the countryside softens and the Coast Range moves inland from the ocean as you travel across undulating marine terraces and through rolling fields of agricultural abundance down the coast through Santa Maria Valley. Just north of Santa Barbara, around Point Conception, the coastal mountains (the Transverse Range) in Santa Barbara County rise boldly with chaparral punctuating the monstrous, jagged rock outcroppings. The flora also transforms radically south of Point Conception—palm trees and bougainvillea proliferate and one thinks of the Mediterranean and Costa del Sol—suddenly you have entered the wonderful realm of Southern California.

Coastal California is by no means limited to the seashore and waterfront resorts. The Coastal kingdom extends inland for many miles. For example, most of California's coastal wine regions such as Monterey, Napa/Sonoma, Paso Robles, San Luis Obispo, and Santa Barbara appellations are located inland from the sea, although they all depend on the Pacific Ocean's environmental influences, such as cooling sea breezes and foggy nights. Many people who make the coastal journey also include inland detours to visit and savor a taste of California's world-renown wineries.

A basic premise of this book is to give the reader ample information about a select group of properties. The common guidebook approach offers the reader a compendium of information, limits each destination to two or three concise paragraphs—but the reader is left teasingly satisfied and minimally informed. Hopefully, after reading each chapter in *Romancing the Coast,* you will know whether or not a particular destination is suited to your personal tastes and sensibilities.

For every destination featured in this edition, there is another equally deserving property that was left on the cutting room floor. The process of elimination was agonizing, but necessary to allow an in-depth description and color photographs of each featured destination.

We offer you a breadth of romantic destinations, from the large, full-service resort properties such as Four Seasons and Ritz Carlton to intimate inns and B&Bs, as well as a few funky and offbeat hideaways such as a night on a yacht or a stay at a Lighthouse in the middle of San Francisco Bay.

Welcome to California's coastal paradise—enjoy your stay!

p.s. I rely on you, the traveler, to let me know about your personal experiences, not only at properties described in this book, but other places that you have loved and enjoyed and would highly recommend. Please feel free to write me (care of the publisher) with your comments, suggestions and thoughts about your personal favorites as well as critical feedback about the destinations described in this book.

Southern California

Hotel Del Coronado

1500 Orange Avenue
Coronado, CA 92118
Telephone: 619-435-6611
Reservations: 1-800-HOTEL-DEL
www.hoteldel.com

Highlights:

♦ The circa-1888 main hotel is a rare California architectural gem with 692 rooms and suites, 26-seaside acres

♦ Mobil Four-Star and AAA Four-Diamond resort

♦ Four-star dining. Ten restaurants and lounges, including The Prince of Whales Grill, rated as "San Diego's most Romantic"

♦ Ideal honeymoon and wedding locale

♦ Handicapped-accessible rooms

♦ Rates in historic Victorian building from $285 to $525, suites from $490 to $1,200. Accommodations in the new oceanside building from $315 to $525, suites from $1,000, inquire about special B&B package.

The Hotel Del Coronado, a California landmark since its debut in 1888, remains as a classic legacy from the flamboyant Gilded Age. The author of *The Wizard of Oz*, L. Frank Baum, frequently spent time at the Del and historians surmise that the Del's fanciful turrets and soaring rooflines inspired Baum's vision of the Land of Oz.

Located on the Coronado Peninsula, across the bay from downtown San Diego, the National Historic Landmark continues its century-long reputation as a premier destination for vacationing families, lovers, honeymooners, and Hollywood stars and starlets. Remember the movie *Some Like It Hot,* starring Marilyn Monroe, Jack Lemmon, and Tony Curtis? Revisit the 1958 film classic and you will see segments filmed on location at the "Del."

Hotel Del Coronado Exterior

And of course, the Del has its obligatory ghost. Soon after Kate Morgan checked into the resort on November 25, 1892 she was found dead in her room, but her spirit lives on in the Del and reports of her spectral appearances continue unabated. If you're a brave soul, request her old room.

The full-scale destination resort is replete with six lighted tennis courts, two heated pools, ten restaurants and lounges, and more than 30 shops and boutiques. If you're in the mood for a massage, there is a complete health, fitness, and massage center.

Fifty million dollars was recently spent on renovations and upgraded interior furnishings, new soft goods and finishes. The historic rooms are individually decorated and feature period antiques. In addition to the original main building there are two newer structures closer to the beach.

Weddings, honeymoons, and anniversaries have been a Del specialty for more than a century and naturally there are numerous onsite locales for ceremonies and receptions. The courtly ballroom overlooking the Pacific is the most popular, but many select open-air settings such as the Garden Patio and oceanfront lawns.

The luxurious "Beach Bungalow" private cottage is the ultra romantic love nest where Marilyn Monroe stayed while filming *Some Like it Hot.* The beachfront bungalow has a large deck, an impressive living room with fireplace, and a separate bedroom. Extra amenities of endearment include breakfast in bed, chocolate covered strawberries and his-and-her massages.

Dining is another star attraction at the Del, from casual bistros and cafés to fine cuisine in the historic Prince of Whales Grill with its floor to ceiling windows and spectacular sunset vistas of the Pacific. The Grill has been proclaimed as San Diego's "Most Romantic Restaurant," the "Best Hotel Dining," and the "Best Sunday Brunch" by *San Diego Magazine.* The adjacent Crown Room is revered for its crown shaped chandeliers and elegant barrel-vaulted wood-paneled ceiling. The Crown is the venue for the weekly Sunday brunch as well as big band and ballroom dancing. The seaside Ocean Terrace restaurant offers al fresco dining and libations in a casual setting.

When you're ready to burn off some calories, there are ample outdoor activities, from surfing and swimming to biking and hiking. The Del's Boathouse is the place to make arrangements for aquatic activities such as fishing excursions, sailboat charters, and whale watching adventures. Golf is available at the adjacent 18-hole Coronado Bayside Golf Course.

The elegant architecture, abundant on-site activities, the oceanfront location, along with its close proximity to downtown San Diego, insures the Del's coveted reputation as California's premier historic seaside resort-destination.

Hotel Del Coronado Dining Room

Hilton San Diego Gaslamp Quarter

401 K Street
San Diego, CA 92101
Telephone: 619-231-4040
Reservations: 800-HILTONS
www.hilton.com

Highlights

♦ Excellent location in Gaslamp Historic Quarter

   Mobil Four Star and AAA Four Diamond resort

♦ Short walk to more than 70 eateries, The Waterfront, Horton Plaza, and Seaport Village

♦ Atesia Day Spa, fitness center, outdoor pool, and sundeck

♦ In-room amenities include down comforters and pillow-top beds, high-quality soaps and shampoos, 25-inch TV, high-speed Internet access and modem hookup, and voicemail and call waiting

♦ The award-winning New Leaf Restaurant's California cuisine and Royale Bar Brasserie's outstanding French cuisine

♦ Eleven handicaped-accessible units

♦ Rates: $199–$3600 (inquire about special packages)

Filtered through windows thirty feet high, a beam of sunlight gently diffuses over an unusually relaxed businessman as he pecks away on his laptop. Nearby, a couple plays chess, warmed by a handsome floor-to-ceiling cherry and maple fireplace. Streamlined stairs beckon to an unexplored second level, where guests can enjoy a large yet inviting loft-style living room where arts and crafts meets urban sophistication. But its practical identity, that of a mezzanine-level lobby, would rarely be guessed. That it arose from a shady past is even more surprising.

In the 1880s, San Diego's Gaslamp District was infamously known as "Stingaree," the red-light district, and home to rough-and-tumble taverns like the Last Chance, the Hole in the Wall Saloon, and the Phoenix. After languishing for nearly a century as a place where steamships were anchored,

HILTON SAN DIEGO GASLAMP QUARTER POOL

Hilton San Diego Gaslamp Quarter Loft

pickles processed, doors milled, and brooms woven, the district has gone through a major economic renaissance—with the cutting-edge Hilton showcasing the reinvented neighborhood.

Boasting an inspiring architectural style that emphasizes soaring spaces, wood-beam ceilings, and ample use of interior brick, this new 282-room hotel establishes an entirely new direction for the Hilton Corporation. Jeremy Cohen, a partner in the project, says, "We are fortunate that Hilton supported us in creating a hotel that is completely different from any Hilton you've ever seen." Different it is, indeed.

A feeling of home permeates each spacious guestroom, from the cozy pillow-top beds with down comforters to the large work desks and complimentary coffee bars. Executive-level accommodations include private concierge service, 300 thread-count Frette linen, continental breakfast, and much more. The recently completed Enclave Wing offers 11 -foot-tall ceilings with spacious loft-style windows.

Within a short-walk's distance are over seventy restaurants, but you don't have to step outside to find fine dining. The on-site Royale Bar Brasserie offers authentic French cuisine with seafood as the house specialty. The operators of the legendary Water Grill in Los Angeles manage this romantic dinner venue. The hotel's other eating establishment, the New Leaf Restaurant,

7

serves creative California cuisine for breakfast, lunch, and dinner; provides in-room dining until 11:00 p.m.; offers an extensive buffet breakfast; and offers, for those balmy days, outdoor deck seating.

Should you need to work out after indulging your appetite, the Hilton is equipped with a whirlpool, heated outdoor pool, and complimentary fitness center (open twenty-four-hours a day) with full cardiovascular and weight-training equipment.

The hotel's Artesia Spa is the place for total body tune-ups. Nature's elements of water and light play throughout the spa's interior, adding the necessary touches for guests to achieve pure repose. In addition to hair styling, pedicures, and manicures, guests can indulge in rejuvenating facials and body treatments. Full-day sessions even include heart-healthy meals prepared by the New Leaf Restaurant.

A myriad of attractions, including Seaport Village, Horton Plaza, the waterfront, and the convention center are within walking distance of the Hilton. For the adventurous, a mere ten-minute drive will deliver you to the legendary San Diego Zoo, Old Town, Balboa Park, Coronado Island, and the San Diego Airport.

The Hilton's unique and alluring Gaslamp Quarter location provides historic charm and all the vibrancy and amenities of today. Stay at this luxurious hotel and indulge in the cozy rooms, accommodating day spa, and award-winning cuisine.

Four Seasons Aviara

7100 Four Seasons Point
Carlsbad, CA 92009
Telephone: 760-603-6800
Reservations: 800-332-3442
www.fourseasons.com/aviara

Highlights

♦ The centerpiece of the award-winning, masterfully planned community of Aviara

♦ AAA Five-Diamond resort

♦ A true destination resort boasting 200 acres, 329 rooms and suites, five restaurants, pool bar and grill, twenty-four-hour room service and five boutiques and gift shops

♦ Health spa offering massage, facial, and body wrap services

♦ Arnold Palmer-designed championship 18-hole golf course

♦ Complete tennis facilities, including six courts lit for night play, tournament seating, lessons, and pro shop

♦ Hilltop setting with vistas of the Batiquitos Lagoon directly below and the ocean in the distance

♦ Handicapped-accessible rooms and facilities

♦ Rates: from $395 to $4,300

As a firm believer in the significance of first impressions setting the tone for memorable stays, the Four Seasons Aviara passed my perquisite test with flying colors. Upon arrival, the valet immediately opened the car door and welcomed me with such sincerity and warmth that I thought, perhaps, he had confused me with someone of import.

The Aviara wins forthright praise for its first-class staff, as well as its

Four Seasons Aviara Spa Solarium

ethereal setting. Situated on a high bluff-top, the resort has a commanding view of the golf course, the Batiquitos Lagoon, the coastal mountains, and the Pacific Ocean in the distance.

The Spanish Colonial and Mission Revival architectural detailing, with smooth plaster walls and red clay-tile roofs, is soothing to the eye and appropriately pays homage to the region's historical roots.

My favorite features are the interior architectural and design elements, such as heavy timber, lightly stained beams and wood paneled ceilings in most of the public spaces. The architects did a commendable job of crafting an inviting sense of "home," paradoxically on a very grand scale. This was done in a manner that does not intimidate or make one feel insignificant, despite the voluminous spaces. For example, the California Bistro—a light and airy, sophisticated but casual dining room with a timbered ceiling—is as inviting and comfortable as being in a friend's living room.

Consistency is a critical ingredient of success at any resort or restaurant, and this is another outstanding Aviara attribute.

The guest rooms (approximately 540 square feet) feature comfy down pillows, perfectly firm beds, outdoor decks and patios with teak table and chairs. There are also in-room coffee makers, safes, irons, Sony Play Station access, two-line telephones, computer/fax data ports, twice-daily maid service and evening turn down. The closets are large enough (seven feet-long) to accommodate a long-term stay, and in the spacious, marble bathrooms you'll find a complete array of luxury soaps and lotions (you know, the type that are just too good to leave behind).

Dining includes Aviara's signature cuisine found in the AAA Four-Diamond winner, Vivace, with its sumptuous northern Italian fare served in a romantic ocean view setting. California Bistro serves breakfast lunch and dinner. Lunch and cocktails are available at the Ocean Pool Bar & Grill, while the Lobby Lounge is the place for afternoon tea, cocktails, and light fare.For the health conscious, all dining venues offer nutritionally balanced "alternative cuisine" selections, which are low in calories, fats, cholesterol, and sodium.

When it comes time for total relaxation, a great place to start is by taking a plunge in the new "Quiet Pool" with its private cabanas and majestic vistas of the lagoon and Pacific beyond. From the pool, move on to the freshly renovated15,000 square-foot Spa for the ultimate indulgence. Services and amenities include steam rooms, saunas, whirlpools, cardio and weight training facilities as well as an assortment of classes from stretching and Pilates to general fitness and power walks. Twenty indoor and five outdoor treatment rooms are used for massage, facials, scrubs, wraps, and more. Additional primping and pampering, including manicures, pedicures, make-up, and hair styling are available in the Jose Eber Salon.

The "spa-widower" is not forsaken at Aviara, as the championship Arnold Palmer golf course offers challenging play amidst 180 acres of wetland-fringed beauty. *Golf Digest* ranks it among the top five new resort courses, and it's also touted as one of the top 50 places to play for women by *Golf Digest Women*.

Aviara is highly recommended for large wedding parties, corporate groups, and vacationing couples. It is also an ideal base-camp for families. Aviara's Kids for All Seasons program allows adults to indulge in grown-up activities while the kids are involved in supervised fun. Designed for children four through twelve years of age, the program offers story telling, games, and videos, and such outdoor educational activities as visits to the Batiquitos Lagoon, sports, races, and swimming.

Aviara is conveniently located within a half-hour of every imaginable San Diego tourist destination, including the San Diego Zoo, California Center for the Arts, Sea World, Balboa Park, Temecula's twelve wineries, Missions San Luis Rey and San Diego de Alcala, and more.

The hilltop oasis of Aviara is one of those idyllic destinations that's awful hard to leave, and the warm remembrances will surley beckon you back long after you've returned home.

FOUR SEASONS AVIARA PALM COURTYARD

Rancho La Valencia Resort

P.O. Box 9126
5921 Valencia Circle
Rancho Santa Fe, CA 92067
Telephone: 858-756-1123
Reservations: 800-548-3664
www.RanchoValencia.com

Highlights

- Forty-acre rural enclave evokes sense of a private luxury estate

- Forty-eight spacious luxury suites and one three-bedroom suite with a full kitchen, private pool, spa, and enclosed garden patio

- Accommodations include oversized bathroom, walk-in closet, wet bar, evening turndown service, fireplace, two TVs, VCR, CD player, and designer bath amenities

- Fresh-squeezed orange juice, newspaper, and rosebud delivered to your doorstep in the morning

- Full-service spa, regulation croquet court, boutique and pro shop, and championship tennis facilities

- In-room spa services include massage, aromatherapy, reflexology, skincare, and manicures and pedicures

- Wedding, meeting, and banquet facilities serve up to 500 guests

- Handicapped-accessible facilities (two ADA approved suites)

- Rates: $435 to $5,000 (per night, double occupancy)

Winding inland from the Pacific, skirting through fields and past luxuriant horse ranches, we motored up a narrow, tree-lined drive and parked under the shade of a sprawling Florida ficus tree. We especially relished our arrival at the tranquil Rancho Valencia Resort after a four-hour drive down the coast.

Rancho Valencia is a lyrical realm of enchantment, washed with lemon, orange, eucalyptus, and palm trees; aromatic honeysuckle; cascading pink

RANCHO VALENCIA RESORT

trumpet-vines; yellow and orange hibiscus; and sanguine-red bougainvillea. Impatiens and agapantha dapple the pathways.

Built in 1989 (with 12 new luxury suites added in 2002), Rancho Valencia is a recent creation, but there's a definitively timeless atmosphere here. This milieu is further instilled through the Spanish Colonial and Mediterranean motifs, saltillo tiles, and authentic red clay garden pots and tiled roofs. The elegant home-like furnishings in the suites and public spaces, the friendly and relaxed manner of the staff, and the quiet setting all serve to make Rancho Valencia a first-class destination for romance—from weddings, honeymoons, and anniversaries to a simple rejuvenation of the bonds of love.

The outstanding culinary experience is reason enough to make a date at Rancho Valencia. Its superlative cuisine has been acknowledged by *Gourmet*

Magazine, while the international wine list has garnered an "Award of Excellence" from *Wine Spectator* for five consecutive years. The main dining room seats 130 people and is supplemented by the Sunrise Room, Palm Room, and the patio courtyard, which offers alfresco seating.

Whether it's breakfast, lunch, or dinner, Rancho Valencia offers a delicious array of tempting menu offerings. A breakfast sampler includes the alternative spa breakfast with such selections as the rancho frittata, made with egg whites, grilled vegetables, sundried tomato, and fresh herbs, and an incredible oat bran waffle with seasonal berries and fresh fruit. Lunch selections include a spicy sautéed crab cake on a bed of shitake mushrooms and a mesclun salad with champagne vinaigrette and pear tomatoes. Mid-day entrees include a spicy Italian sausage calzone with caramelized sweet onions and baked Chilean sea bass wrapped in spinach, served in puff pastry with young vegetables in a lemon-butter sauce. Dinner entrées include a delicious sautéed imported Magret duck breast served with roasted potatoes, green peppercorns, and a black cherry balsamic sauce. Equally enticing is the pan-roasted veal chop with Valencia garden herb gnocchi and grilled portobello mushrooms with Madeira demi-cream sauce.

Rancho Valencia Resort Hacienda Pool

Rancho Valencia offers a complete array of cardiovascular workout equipment and cutting-edge massage and beauty facilities. Spa services include Swedish, Shiatsu, aromatic target, and arnica sports massage. In-room treatments are a highly recommended house specialty, eliminating the need to dress and walk back to your room after a soothing massage.

Rancho Valencia, an ideal destination for corporate retreats, also attracts glitterati in pursuit of unfettered relaxation. Notable guests in the recent past include Dennis Miller, President Clinton, Rene Russo, Jenny Craig, Michael Jordan, Woody Harrelson, Regis Philbin, and Bill Blass. As an historical aside, the resort adjoins the former estate of Hollywood screen idols Mary Pickford and Douglas Fairbanks, who dubbed their 800-acre hideaway "Rancho Zorro."

Rancho Valencia's award-winning tennis facility (ranked among the top ten tennis resorts in the U.S. by *Tennis Magazine*) is spread over the resort in an impressive garden setting. Tennis amenities include eighteen Plexipave hard-surface courts (one with an automated serving machine), a center court with spectator seating, and tennis clinics for all ages and skills offered daily by U.S.P.T.A certified professionals.

Rancho Valencia offers golf privileges at four nearby championship golf courses with driving ranges and pro shops. Additional offsite activities include hiking, biking, hot-air-balloon rides, polo, wine tasting, and more.

If there were no on-site amenities and you never ventured beyond the confines of your suite and garden patio, a stay at Rancho Valencia would still remain an incredibly satisfying and memorable experience. From the tranquil setting, homey abodes, delectable cuisine, and sophisticated spa services, to the world-class tennis facilities and the professional, friendly staff, Rancho Valencia is a highly recommended destination for love and romance or for that simple and much needed refreshment of the mind, body, and spirit.

La Valencia Hotel

1132 Prospect Street
La Jolla, California 92037
Telephone: 858-454-0771
Reservations: 800-451-0772
www.LaValencia.com

Highlights

♦ Picturesque location in the heart of downtown La Jolla

♦ Heated pool, jacuzzi, and a fitness center equipped with a dry sauna and massage room, on-site bicycle rentals

♦ Custom designed bath amenities, plush terry cloth bathrobes, cable TV and VCRs, turndown service

♦ Valet parking, bilingual concierge service, 24-hour room service

♦ The Spa Alliance offers a full array of massage, facials, manicures, and pedicures

♦ Member, National Trust Historic Hotels of America

♦ Handicapped-accessible rooms and facilities

♦ Rates: rooms and suites from $300 to $1,300; luxury Ocean Villas from $775 to $3,500

Located on a bluff above a sweeping blue curve of glittering Pacific Ocean sits La Jolla's "Pink Lady." More formally known as La Valencia, the Mediterranean-style hotel is endowed with a rich history and a casually elegant ambiance that has made it one of the most beloved seaside resorts in the world.

La Valencia was Truman Capote's favorite hotel. And that's saying a lot, for he traveled widely, often living and writing for long periods of time in suites from Italy to Ischia, from New Orleans to New York.

LA VALENCIA HOTEL

Just 12 miles from San Diego International airport, the hotel has been casting a spell on its guests ever since it opened in 1926. Back in the day, Groucho Marx, Lillian Gish, and Mary Pickford were frequent guests.

Even though the hotel has been freshly renovated and updated with the latest amenities, it still retains its old-world charm, particularly in the 15 ocean villas. These cozy retreats are perfect for couples looking for privacy, relaxation, and the breezy romance of sultry nights.

Below the hotel is Ellen Browning Scripps Park, a popular spot for picnics, strolling, jogging, and colorful sunset views. There is nothing quite like an afternoon spent in the salty air and abundant sunshine to sharpen one's appetite, and La Valencia has four fine restaurants to satisfy a variety of tastes and moods.

The Whaling Bar, part of the hotel's post-WWII renovations, has a warm, clubby atmosphere. Small and intimate, its plush red-leather booths, ivory scrimshaw, and wood paneling attract patrons who like to "power" lunch and unwind during cocktail hour.

The Sky Room is more formal, specializing in fine French cuisine with an extensive wine list. The Kobe beef carpaccio with baby artichokes is a favorite here. The Sky Room offers the ultimate in romantic dining with only 12 booths and tables, each overlooking La Jolla Cove.

The Mediterranean Room and Tropical Patio is suited to all occasions. Catch a cool breeze or enjoy the sunshine while dining or sipping a drink alfresco. La Sala, located in the rear of the lobby, is a cozy place to unwind and people-watch while enjoying a casual cocktail. Note the unique hand-painted ceiling and impressive floor-to-ceiling windows overlooking the Pacific.

And then there's the swimming pool, with its comfortable deck chairs, crystalline blue waters, and the shade of surrounding palm trees. It's a leafy oasis, one of the many features that convince some guests that there's no reason to leave the hotel.

La Valencia Hotel is a gracious getaway for couples seeking a taste of old California melded with the new.

LA VALENCIA LA SALA

L'Auberge Del Mar Resort and Spa

1540 Camino Del Mar at 15th Street
Del Mar, California 92014
Telephone: 858-259-1515
Reservations: 800-553-1336
www.laubergedelmar.com

Highlights

♦ Romantic seaside setting, steps from the beach, boutique shopping, restaurants, and galleries

♦ Mobil Four Star and AAA Four-Diamond resort

♦ 120 rooms, including eight suites, many with private balconies

♦ Complete European-style health spa, indoor and outdoor fitness pavillion

♦ Two lighted tennis courts (on-site pro), swimming pools—leisure and lap

♦ J. Taylor's of Del Mar for fine California dining

♦ Excellent wedding, anniversary, and honeymoon venue

♦ Romance Director to advise and guide couples on romantic opportunities

♦ Five ADA accessible rooms

♦ Rates from $245 to $1,600

Monday through Thursday, L'Auberge does a thriving trade with small corporate meetings and retreats, but when the weekend rolls around the driving force here is love, romance, weddings, and anniversaries. Some people check in expressly to relax and indulge while others are attracted by the litany of specialized European spa treatments, the fine cuisine and attentive service.

L'AUBERGE PACIFIC TERRACE

Built on the site of the legendary Hotel Del Mar where film legends such as Pickford, Fairbanks, and Chaplin came to play, the new L'Auberge (opened in 1989) continues the tradition. Don't be surprised if you find Bonnie Raitt, Bruce Willis, or Demi Moore waltzing around the property or Jane Seymour and Connie Chung relaxing in the spa.

L'Auberge provides a perfect blend of the sophisticated amenities found at a full-blown resort destination blended with the intimate, attentive service of a boutique property. For those seeking the ideal romantic experience, L'Auberge is amply prepared—you see, in addition to the customary guest relations staff, there's also a Director of Romance.

Nancy Hirsch has been working at L'Auberge Del Mar since it opened and there's very little she doesn't know about anything on the property or in Del Mar or San Diego County. In addition to overseeing concierge services at the L'Auberge, Hirsch is the person to see if you're planning a wedding, a honeymoon or just an extra special romantic getaway. Hirsch's extensive lexicon of romantic activities includes: arranging for an aerial skywriter to scrawl a romantic message across the sky at sunset, scheduling a hot air balloon adventure, or sending you off in a limo for a day of wine tasting.

When you come to stay at the L'Auberge, park your car and forget about it until it's time to depart. Numerous attractions are within easy walking distance. The beach and bluff tops are literally right out front while the legendary Torrey Pines State Reserve is only three miles away. There is also whale watching, mountain biking, hiking, golf, and more close by.

Many savvy South Coast foodies regard J. Taylor's of Del Mar at the L'Auberge as the foremost dining venue in the Del Mar area. Named after a founding father of Del Mar, J. Taylor's recently completed a half-million dollar renovation. It retained some of the classical elements while infusing a residential flair. The decor is casually elegant, with a cracking fireplace, orchids, cathedral ceilings, and French doors opening to a courtyard.

California regional cuisine is the guiding light in the kitchen and ample use of fresh herbs and local farm-fresh produce are essential ingredients.

The 120 guestrooms (including eight luxurious suites) feature high-quality custom interior finishes, telephone dataports, wet bars, marble baths, and private balconies or patios.

At the spa, the signature L'Auberge treatments are among the most requested services. The Pacific Paradise Body Scrub and Massage is tops. The treatment includes California grape seed as an anti-oxidant defoliant body scrub, followed by a pineapple papaya moisturizer. Inquire about special overnight spa packages.

From the beguiling seaside setting to the indulgent spa treatments, fine dining and attentive staff, L'Auberge Del Mar Resort and Spa is one of those special places where lifetime memories are born and nurtured.

The Inn at Rancho Santa Fe

PO Box 869
5951 Linea del Cielo
Rancho Santa Fe, CA 92067
Telephone: 858-756-1131
Reservations: 800-THE-INNI (843-4661)
www.theinnatranchosantafe.com

Highlights

♦ A step back in time to 1930s and '40s California

♦ Tranquil garden grounds with red-tile roofed cottages, standard rooms and suites

♦ Wood-burning fireplaces, decks, and kitchenettes

♦ Three tennis courts, swimming pool, croquet

♦ Fine dining, pub, library, and grand living room

♦ Nearby championship golf and legendary Del Mar race track, hot air ballooning, wine tasting, biking, shopping

♦ Two handicapped accessible rooms

♦ Rates: Standard cottages, $210 to $800

What an understated, seductive sanctuary. You will not find a hint of flamboyant gaudiness at the Inn at Rancho Santa Fe. What you will find is an oasis of tranquility and simplicity, personified through its classic board-and-batten sided cottages with red-clay tile roofs. The main lodge building contains the reception area, a cozy pub, library, and dining room as well as corporate offices and guestrooms.

Most memorable and outstanding is the ingratiating sense that you have entered a time warp—nothing of import has been changed or altered markedly since the inn opened in 1941. Historic photos framed on the walls of the inn boldly testify to the *Twilight Zone* aspect of the inn and

RANCHO SANTA FE FRONT ENTRANCE

the village of Rancho Santa Fe. The focal point of the public space is the grand living room with its soaring vaulted ceiling accented with intricately carved corbels and timber beams, vintage multi-pane wood French doors, and smooth plastered walls. Throughout the living room there are vintage ship models, artworks and furnishings as well as a beckoning traditional fireplace—engagingly reflective of the long-vanished Spanish and Mexican colonial era in California del Norte.

It is only 20 miles to San Diego, but once you unpack and settle in to your cottage, you'll quickly forget that there's a city anywhere—or for that matter, what decade it is. Accommodations vary, ranging from standard rooms, suites with wood-burning fireplaces and kitchenettes, to spacious freestanding cottages. The lushly foliated grounds enhance the sense of being encapsulated in a very private, insular cocoon world of your own.

The village of Rancho Santa Fe, replete with upscale boutique shops and excellent eateries, is one of the cutest and quaintest little burgs in all of Southern California. The town also holds title as one of the wealthiest communities in the entire United States. The rambling estates are sometimes mistaken by guests arriving for the first time at the Inn. An arriving guest recently called the front desk from their cell-phone to inquire if someone might be kind enough to unlock the entry gate. The clerk responded with a chuckle, "We don't have a gate. You must be parked in front of someone's private home," and proceeded to redirect them to the little Inn with 87 bedrooms.

Nearby activities include golf at Rancho Santa Fe Golf Club, The Meadows Del Mar, Morgan Run Resort & Club, Maderas Golf Club, the Vineyard, Encinitas Ranch, Aviara, and Torrey Pines (green fees range from around $50 to $200). World famous Del Mar racetrack is not far away and the Inn offers guests box seats and turf club passes.

The 87 guest accommodations include 14 suites and private cottages. Many of the rooms have private patios, decks, kitchenettes, wood burning fireplaces and wet bars, while all are graced with handsome furnishings (many antiques) and original artworks on the walls.

If you're coming to stay for more than a night or two, inquire about the Inn's private beach cottage (providing showers, dressing rooms, and a private patio) right on the waterfront at Del Mar Beach.

On-site amenities include fine dining (breakfast, lunch, and dinner), banquet facilities, corporate meeting spaces (up to 200 theater-style), three tennis courts, an elegant swimming pool, Jacuzzi spa, croquet court, and fitness room.

The Lodge at Torrey Pines

11480 Torrey Pines Road
La Jolla, CA 92037
Telephone: 858-453-4420
Reservations: 800-656-0087
www.lodgetorreypines.com

Highlights

♦ One of coastal California's newest resorts, opened spring 2002

♦ Exquisite architectural detailing capture classic Arts and Crafts elements

♦ 170 rooms, two restaurants

♦ Onsite 9,500-square-foot spa

♦ Golf pro shop, driving range, and course adjacent to the Lodge

♦ Miles of hiking trails and pristine beaches nearby

♦ Handicapped-accessible rooms and facilities

♦ Rates from $375, suites from $900

Several hundred years ago, early Spanish explorers used the Punto de Los Arboles (Point of the Trees) as a navigational landmark while the sailors traversed the Southern California coastline. Today, however, the majestic grove of Ice-Age-relic pines provides not only a stunning backdrop for one of golf's most legendary venues, the Torrey Pines Golf Course, but also lends its beauty to one of Southern California's newest and most luxurious destinations, The Lodge at Torrey Pines.

Unveiled in spring of 2002, the Lodge is a perfectly detailed tribute to early-1900s Craftsman design. The Lodge's hand-crafted detailing and outstanding artisanship are evidenced throughout the 175 guest rooms, generous meeting and banquet spaces, two restaurants, and 9,500 square foot full-service spa.

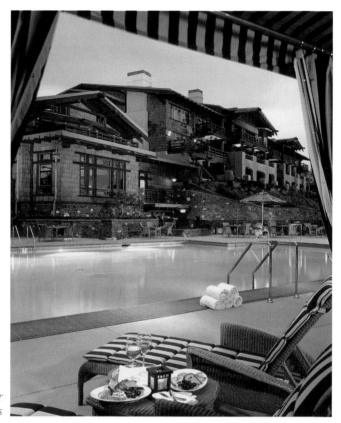

THE LODGE AT
TORREY PINES

Reflecting the Craftsman Movement's passion for honest materials, respect for natural landscape, and integration of interior and exterior elements, the Lodge's exterior features powerful post-and-beam construction, expanses of nature-inspired stained glass, shingle and sandstone facades and graceful, wing-like rooflines. Inside, Greene brother's inspired light fixtures softly illuminate living-room-like groupings of Stickly furniture nestled on Oriental rugs in the heavy-timbered lobby, while California Impressionist landscapes dot the walls to complete the effect. And, of course, guest rooms also observe the Craftsman detailing—from the custom-designed furniture's inlaid-wood Arts and Crafts motifs to oil-rubbed bronze fixtures and rich leather chaise lounges—all contributing their allegiance to elegance and warmth.

Rooms range in size from 520 square feet to more than 1,500 square feet and command views of either the links or the Lodge's indigenous-flora-lined central courtyard.

A guest's sense of tranquility is further augmented by The Spa's traditional, therapeutic treatments, which are enhanced by local products in an exquisite setting.

The Lodge offers several distinct settings to satisfy gustatory demands. The casual-dining restaurant, The Grill, is the perfect place for enjoying breakfast, lunch, and healthful, light snacks—offerings similar to those found at The Lodge's two comfortable lounges as well. But it is the signature restaurant, A.R.Valentien, that promises fulfillment at an entirely different level. Poised in a breathtaking setting overlooking the Torrey Pine's 18th green, the restaurant takes advantage of all that California has to offer.

After a fine meal or relaxing massage, The Lodge offers guests still more in the way of recreational activities. The outdoor pool and whirlpool spa might beckon some, while others may choose to explore the Torrey Pines State Reserve's miles of walking trails through rare forests, or sunbathe and perhaps even swim at its pristine beaches. And for golf aficionados, The Lodge offers hotel guests guaranteed tee times and special golf packages. The golf pro shop, driving range, and golf school are also adjacent to the lodge.

The Lodge at Torrey Pines

The Ritz-Carlton, Laguna Niguel

One Ritz-Carlton Drive
Dana Point, CA 92629
Telephone: 949-240-2000
Reservations: 800-241-3333
www.ritzcarlton.com

Highlights

- Spectacular seaside setting from atop a 150-foot bluff

- Mobil Five-Star and AAA Five-Diamond resort

- Jogging and bicycle trails and two miles of broad, sandy beach

- Eighteen-hole Robert Trent Jones golf course adjacent to property

- Four tennis courts with on-site pro

- Health spa with full array of offerings, including deep tissue massage, aromatherapy, co-ed steam room, heated pools, and Jacuzzi tubs

- Four fine dining and casual restaurants and a private wine-and-dine room that accommodates up to twelve people

- Handicapped accessible facilities and thirteen handicapped accessible rooms

- Rates from $375 to $475; Ritz Club Level rooms and suites from 495 to $3,500

The Ritz-Carlton, Laguna Niguel is an amazing place. It manages to fuse a delightful balance of the laid-back lifestyle that pervades southern California with the very best of Old World sensibilities.

The atmosphere is casual, relaxed, and unpretentious; yet there's also an underlying element of things refined and discrete, gracious and charming. The Ritz at Laguna Niguel reminds me of an acquaintance who is the CEO of a major international corporation. He dines with kings and queens and

The Ritz Carlton, Laguna Niguel

meets with high-ranking executives in Monte Carlo and Cairo, but he also loves to get out and surf with his beach buddies on Wednesday afternoons.

The Ritz seems to do everything with stately perfection, and it is no coincidence that Laguna Niguel claims the coveted Five-Star award from Mobil, as well as AAA's distinguished Five-Diamond status. The four-story, Mediterranean-flavored Ritz Laguna Niguel also consistently wins world-class rankings in annual *Condé Nast* reader polls and numerous other international travel journals.

What exactly is it that makes the Ritz so outstanding? Everything. The employees are bright, alert, and anticipatory, yet discrete in manner and attitude. The culinary offerings and presentation are suitable for a *Gourmet Magazine* cover shot. The accommodations are luxurious, as are the manicured grounds and interior spaces.

The Ritz is also home to one of California's most exquisite private fine art collections. The works grace the walls of the public spaces and hallways throughout the resort. Every week, the Ritz hosts a special "Discover the Arts" guided tour, followed by a three-course meal in the Restaurant-162.

A truly priceless ingredient at the Ritz is the oceanfront setting. I never tired of sitting on the outdoor deck of my room and gazing out across the sea toward Santa Catalina Island, watching the surfers ride six-foot waves.

The Ritz is prepared for its beach-going guests and offers complimentary use of beach equipment, including umbrellas, beach towels, fins, snorkel masks, beach chairs, and boogie boards. During the summer months, beach shuttle service runs on the hour.

Among the long list of five-star touches are twice daily maid service with turndown in the evening, fully stocked honor bars, color TVs with complimentary movie channel, in-room safes, terry cloth robes, and lavish Italian marble in the baths, which are equipped with double vanities. Other distinguishing comforts include a complete business center, golf bag and luggage storage facilities, gift shops, hair salon, same-day laundry, overnight shoe shine, on-site limousine and car rental service, valet parking, transportation to and from Los Angeles International Airport and San Diego's Lindbergh Field, foreign currency exchange, and more.

Rooms in the Ritz-Carlton Club wing come with so many extra services and benefits that they are probably a better value than the regular rooms. The Club level has limited key access. A private concierge is on duty throughout the day and evening to assist you with any personal requests or needs. I was most impressed with the ever-changing array of food, hors d'oeuvres,

The Ritz Carlton Laguna Niguel Suite

afternoon tea service, evening cocktails, soft drinks, and after dinner sweets that were always elegantly arranged on a serving table and side bar. The presentations were exceptionally generous and delicious.

The Ritz is quite suitable for vacationing families. There is a special Ritz Kids daycare program that offers a wide variety of engaging activities for children six through twelve years of age. Situated halfway between Los Angeles and San Diego, the Ritz is within close proximity to a zillion things to do and see. For example, Mission San Juan Capistrano is only five minutes away, Laguna Beach Artist Colony is just ten minutes away, Disneyland and Knotts Berry Farm are within forty minutes, and Santa Catalina Island is just a one-hour boat ride from Laguna Beach.

Whether the occasion is a wedding, honeymoon, family vacation, or corporate event, the Ritz-Carlton, Laguna Niguel is an ideal destination: a five-star resort for five-star memories.

Montage Resort and Spa

30801 South Coast Highway
Laguna Beach, CA 92651
Telephone: 949-715-6000
Reservations: 888-715-6700
www.montagelagunabeach.com

Highlights

- Spectacular oceanfront setting complements timeless Craftsman architecture

- Mobil Four Star and AAA Four Diamond resort

- Museum-quality fine art, sculpture, and ceramics collection

- 20,000-square-foot oceanfront spa offers comprehensive and a la carte treatments as well as fitness programs

- 262 guestrooms, including 51 suites and 37 beach cottages, all with either private balconies or porches

- Thirty lushly landscaped beachfront acres

- Montage's signature restaurant, Studio, and more casual venues including The Loft, Mosaic Grille, and Lobby Lounge

- Swimming pools, croquet lawn, artist's cove, snorkeling, kayaking, surfing, beach volleyball, art classes, yoga, tai chi, and aerobics

- On-site marine biologist acquaints guests with site's natural history and marine life

- Two nearby, Tom Faze-designed golf courses

- Ten handicapped-accessible rooms

- Rates from $599 to $6,000

The Montage Resort and Spa Loft Breakfast

The Montage Resort and Spa, the first luxury seaside property to open in Laguna Beach in 50 years, creates the ultimate romantic getaway. The sun-splashed circular driveway lined with bristling bougainvillea and the crisp ocean air are a wonderful welcome to weary travelers—or anyone who just needs a break from the ordinary weekend getaway. Guests are offered champagne upon arrival and then escorted directly to their rooms. Cognizant of the fact that arriving guests may have just concluded a tiring transcontinental journey, registration formalities are taken care of en suite—a much-appreciated touch.

High above the Pacific, the bluff-top Studio is not to be missed. Using the region's fresh and healthful ingredients, his dishes impress even the most discriminating food critics.

The chef welcomes diners into his small but immaculate kitchen, inviting them to pull up a chair at a comfy banquette, sip a glass of wine and watch the kitchen staff do their thing. It's food-preparation voyeurism—just like on the Food Channel—only without the cameras. The chef says, "We get from ten to thirty-five people a night strolling through or sitting and watching us work." The acclaimed patissier baked goods alone are worth a visit to the Montage's sumptuous Sunday brunch. You can sample his pastries in abundance with other deliciously decadent desserts, including the special chocolate concoctions that have earned him ranking as one of the "Top Ten Pastry Chefs in America" by *Chocolatier* magazine.

The Montage's interior is as impressive as its breathtaking natural setting. The lobby features stunning cherry-wood marquetry flanked by two marble check-in areas. Distinctive period elements, such as classic wood and stone architecture, crown molding, and rich, dark wood create the resort's Craftsman-style design that reflects the California Arts and Crafts Movement of the early 1900s.

The Montage has three specialty shops, each offering a distinctive theme. The Art of Writing sells fine European papers, pens, leather journals, and other writing materials, while The Art of Fragrance, next door, offers exclusive perfumes, soaps, and lotions. Treasures offers men's and women's clothing, including women's apparel by Trina Turk, an exclusive Santa Monica designer who has created a buzz in the fashion world from L.A. to New York.

After a long day of exploring sun, surf, and the resort's hidden treasures, guest rooms serve as a haven of quilted comfort. Turn-of-the-century style rooms tranquilize the soul. Each guestroom has a private balcony and ocean view, providing that soothing background lull that's conducive to a refreshing nap or good night's sleep. Additional amenities include flat-screen TVs, CD and DVD players, and French bath soaps and lotions.

The 262 guest rooms include 51 suites, ranging from 800 to 2,800 square feet, and 37 bungalow-style rooms. But the visit wouldn't be complete without a final bit of pampering at the spa. From conventional thirty-minute Swedish neck and shoulder massages to the more modern ocean-inspired therapies, such as the algae cellulite massage or the thalasso bath, Spa Montage has a variety of treatments that are sure to rid your body of that last bit of remaining stress.

Casual yet elegant, upscale but never stuffy, the Montage strikes a perfect balance of elements and amenities that only the finest resorts can offer. This symphonic medley of sensations to soothe the heart, mind, and soul will leave you relaxed and invigorated.

Inn at Laguna Beach

211 North Coast Highway
Laguna Beach, CA 92651
Telephone: 949-497-9722
Reservations: 800-544-4479
www. innatlagunabeach.com

Highlights

- True seaside property with 52 ocean view and 18 village view rooms

- Mobil Three-Star and AAA Three-Diamond resort

- Excellent base camp for discovering Laguna's numerous upscale art galleries, restaurants, and trendy specialty shops

- Swimming pool, Jacuzzi, complimentary use of beach umbrellas, beach towels

- Complimentary Continental breakfast and newspaper delivered to your room

- Five handicapped-accessible units

- Rates from $129 to $549. Winter rates slightly lower January through May 22. Inquire about special off-season packages and corporate rates.

As I turned into the front entryway from The Pacific Coast Highway, I wasn't sure if the Inn at Laguna Beach was on the waterfront, or if the rooms even had a view of the sea. But once I stepped into the foyer, I was immediately struck by the sight through the glass doors on the far side of the reception area. The vista was reminiscent of a shimmering pastel watercolor that deftly captures all the consummate qualities that you associate with a Southern California beach town—broad, curving beach, umbrellas, surfers, lifeguard stand, and kids shoveling sand.

Situated in the heart of the seaside village of Laguna Beach, the inn is perched on the edge of a sheer bluff. Directly below, the waves explode in a never-ending symphony of thunderous applause.

INN AT LAGUNA BEACH POOL

By the time I rode the elevator up to my fifth floor ocean-view room, I already understood why this inn is so popular—people come here to savor the setting. The feather duvet, CD player, TV/VCR, in-room coffeemaker, and so on, merely make the experience that much more comfortable and enticing. Ninety percent of the rooms are nearly the same in square footage and features, but the price of a room increases in direct proportion to the awesomeness of the view.

For myself, I've become so enamored with my room-with-a-view that as I write these words to the accompaniment of waves crashing below, I find that I don't want this moment to end. Unfortunately, check-out time is fast-approaching. I suppose that's a perfect test of a great getaway—wishing you could stay for just one more day, or even one more hour.

Grand Californian Hotel
at Disneyland

1600 South Disneyland Drive
Anaheim, CA 92803
Reservations: 714-635-2300
www.disneyland.disney.go.com

Highlights

♦ Dramatic design cleverly captures elements of the American Arts and Crafts and Craftsman movements

♦ AAA Four-Diamond location

♦ Four-star amenities, including twenty-four-hour room service, concierge service, valet parking, and evening children's activities

♦ Napa Rose Restaurant featuring fine cuisine and excellent wine list

♦ Eureka Springs Health Club with massage, steam rooms, and fitness center

♦ Twenty-three handicapped-accessible rooms

♦ Rates: standard rooms from $190 to $330; suites from $370; presidential suites from $2,165 to $2,575

For some reason, the adjectives "exotic, romantic, and sophisticated" just don't come to mind when you imagine Disneyland as a prospective destination. But take one step under the broad porte-cochere at the Grand Californian Hotel, and you'll quickly begin to understand.

Disneyland "imagineers" did a masterful job, and at unimaginable expense, crafting a seductive niche in the competitive realm of upscale vacation-destinations when they dreamt up the impressive Grand Californian Hotel. Architects, interior designers, and landscape artists combined talents to integrate classic Arts and Crafts and Craftsman motifs with the Golden State's best attributes. Floor-to-ceiling windows on the Great Hall's north

Grand Californian Hotel at Disneyland

side frame a dreamy vista of redwoods and Monterey Pines while its south side captures plants and trees found in the southern part of the state.

The Grand Californian houses 751 rooms, including two palatial Presidential Suites, two Vice Presidential Suites and 34 exotic Artisan Suites. In-room amenities, from standard rooms to luxury suites, include daily laundry and evening turndown services, Italian marble vanities, coffee makers, mini-bars, robes, irons, hair dryers, and morning newspaper. The first Disney hotel to be built within a Disney theme park, The Grand Californian is literally one step away from the gate leading to the new California Experience theme park and just a hop and a skip from the original Disneyland.

When it's time to dine at the Grand Californian, you're in for another pleasant treat. Once again, no expense was spared in the creation of Napa Rose—the elegant four-star dining destination that celebrates California's legendary wines and stellar agricultural offerings. Napa Rose is a dazzling space in a half-oval design with 20-foot-tall vaulted ceilings. In addition to the 237-seat main dining room, there is an elegant lounge and handsome private dining room with a fireplace and floor-to-ceiling windows overlooking a tranquil garden patio. The restaurant offers more than 50 wines by the glass and a selection of 300 vintages, highlighting California's premier wine producers. *Zagat Guide* rated Napa Rose as Orange County's number one restaurant, and there are twenty-six certified sommeliers on staff.

Storytellers Café, a family friendly establishment, features American contemporary cuisine. Colorful six-foot murals, depicting scenes from classic children's stories, decorate the walls. Of note is the bountiful breakfast buffet and cooking islands where kids can watch chefs prepare their meals.

Though Disneyland is synonymous with children and families, there's a parallel universe where romantic couples are equally enchanted by the Disney experience. The Grand Californian does a masterful job of catering to the diverse needs and sensitivities of all guests. From intimate weddings to grand affairs of more than 1,200 guests, the Grand Californian's Fairy Tale Wedding Coordinators at Bridal Salon can make your every wish and whim come true.

Ready for the engagement of a lifetime? Sleeping Beauty's Royal Engagement ceremony takes place in the Magic Kingdom after hours. Royal Coachmen escort the couple to Cinderella's crystal coach for a jaunt down Main Street to Sleeping Beauty Castle where heralds welcome the pre-nuptial couple with regal fanfare. The couple is then escorted to Snow White's wishing well by the Fairy Godmother, where they will find a bouquet of roses and a glass slipper containing the engagement rings. Subsequently, Mickey and Minnie Mouse and a strolling violinist lead the couple to the Castle Garden where a starlit five-course dinner awaits. The evening closes with a ride back down Main Street in Cinderella's crystal coach.

GRAND CALIFORNIAN HOTEL AT DISNEYLAND LOBBY

Dockside Boat & Bed Long Beach

Dock 5 - Rainbow Harbor
Long Beach, CA 90802
Telephone: 562-436-3111
Reservations: 800-436-2574
www.boatandbed.com

Highlights

♦ Play Onassis for the day—a whimsical change of pace from a landlocked B&B

♦ Romantic packages include onboard massage, long stem roses, chocolate-dipped strawberries, champagne, and more await your arrival

♦ Handicapped accessible

♦ Rates from $175 to $300. Includes continental breakfast with an assortment of pastries, danish, croissants, orange juice, coffee, and tea delivered to your yacht

There you are, floating lazily on the bay, the sun is just starting to dip down. You're sipping martinis, lounging on the transom of your yacht. In the near distance is the Long Beach skyline. Across the harbor, the stately mother ship, Queen Mary, slumbers regally at her permanent berth.

Boat and Bed—what a great concept! Dockside Boat & Bed is like the beach-cabin rental system of boatdom. Owners put their yachts in the Boat & Bed stable and people come to stay on the yachts for the night, or two or three. The yacht owner staunches his financial hemorrhage and we get to play Onassis for the day.

A delightful aspect of an overnight stay on a Dockside Boat is that you're snuggled in your private yacht floating on the water—but you are only one step from shore. Although, you might never leave your waterborne abode once you're settled in. The yachts, ranging in length from 44-foot to 60-foot, include sailboats and full motor vessels, and even an authentic Chinese Junk.

Dockside Boat & Bed view

There is something inherently romantic about yachts. Dockside does a splendid business with the love-bird set, and they are ready with an array of special romance packages, including the Romantic Dinner Package. At $295 per couple, it includes one night accommodation on the yacht of your choice, champagne served upon check-in, dinner for two at La Traviata (a nearby romantic Italian restaurant) and a bottle of house wine, taxi service to and from the restaurant, overnight parking and continental breakfast served on the boat in the morning. Price includes tax, tip, and gratuities.

How about two 45-minute massages in the privacy of your yacht, complete with soothing music and aromatherapy candles? If unraveling the stresses and knots from your work week require more serious attention, Dockside is prepared to cure all that ails you by sending you off down the gangplank to a nearby Day Spa.

Located directly across the bay from the historic Queen Mary, many Dockside guests take the water taxi over to the big boat for an alternate dining venue and the Queen's legendary Sunday Brunch.

A mere ten-minute drive from Dockside Boat & Bed is the romantic Gondola Getaways, offering authentic gondola rides through the canals of Naples, a small waterfront-neighborhood in Long Beach. The rides are approximately $55 per hour and come complete with cheese, salami, bread as well as a singing gondolier.

The Regent Beverly Wilshire

9500 Wilshire Boulevard
Beverly Hills, CA 90212
Telephone: 310-275-5200
Reservations: 800-421-4354
www.fourseasons.com

Highlights:

- Unparalleled location at the foot of Rodeo Drive at Wilshire Boulevard
- Landmark building with European architecture and grand marble lobby
- Sumptuous Dining Room, elegant Lobby Lounge and The Bar
- Spa and Fitness Center
- Mediterranean-style outdoor pool with whirlpool
- Large marble bathrooms with deep-soaking tubs and separate shower in each room
- World-renowned reputation for its legendary history, outstanding service and style
- Nineteen ADA Handicapped-accessible rooms
- Rates from $435 for standard rooms, suites from $650 to $950, Presidential Suite $5,500, Penthouse Suite $7,500

In the mid sixties, about the time he was making the now-classic film *Bonnie and Clyde,* Warren Beatty checked into the Regent Beverly Wilshire. The legendary Lothario liked it so much he checked out ten years later.

This haute hotel has a softly glamorous glow, skillfully blending the best of trendy and traditional elegance with impeccable service in the heart of Beverly Hills. Built in 1928, this E-shaped Italian Renaissance-style edifice is located at the world's most illustrious intersection: Rodeo Drive and Wilshire Boulevard, a springboard to some of the best shopping in the world.

REGENT BEVERLY WILSHIRE POOL

Our visit commenced in the Lobby Lounge, a serene and stylish oasis, where we lingered over a satisfying Afternoon Tea. Nestled in a plush sofa, we listen to the soothing sounds of a pianist while enjoying a fragrant cup tea.

The Regent's comfortable bars and lounges are ideal for intimate tete-a-tetes, but for grander occasions there is the 15,000-square-foot ballroom, one of the most beautiful in the city, which has hosted Prince Charles, former President Clinton (who played the saxophone on stage with B.B. King at a charity event), Paul McCartney, N'Synch, Elton John, Sting, and numerous other notables, from rockers to royalty.

A stroll through the palatial lobby and zigzagging arcade of fine shops provided some pleasantly opulent amusement before we settled into a cozy corner table in the hotel's award-winning restaurant for our evening meal.

The Restaurant's stylish décor has won numerous awards and it's easy to see why. Rich mahogany and satinwood paneled walls accented with Murano glass chandeliers suspended from trompe l'oeil painted ceilings create a grandly elegant setting that is never overpowering or intimidating. Like all the dining venues at the Regent Beverly Wilshire, it shines with chic sophistication while maintaining a cozy ambiance.

It is a popular spot with locals, always a good sign, so you might catch a glimpse of a celebrity. As we were leaving, we spotted a dapper Burt Reynolds at the head of a large table, entertaining a casual group of jovial companions.

Adjacent to the dining room is the Lobby Bar, a swanky hideaway with a first-class light-fare menu that ranges from fried calamari and pizza to salads and sandwiches.

Every corner of this Hollywood hideaway seems to offer a uniquely memorable amenity, including the elevators. It was the unusually located settees that prompted Julia Roberts in *Pretty Woman,* which was filmed here, to squeal with delight, "Color me happy, there's a seat in the elevator."

But the elevators are only a foreshadowing of the exceptional luxury suites, which are understated and oversized, ranging from the 725-square-foot Regency Suite, with mountain and skyline views, to the staggeringly capacious 3,500 square-foot antique-filled Presidential Suite.

The hotel is divided into two parts, each a unique environment. The historic Wilshire Wing, the original part of the hotel that dates back to 1928, appeals to more classic tastes. But equally appealing is the Beverly Wing, a recent addition, with stunning contemporary elegance and modern conveniences that include advanced telecommunications, spacious bathrooms of Italian tile and marble with separate showers and soaking tubs.

REGENT BEVERLY WILSHIRE LOBBY

Just when we thought the hotel couldn't offer any more surprises, we realized that we'd just scratched the surface. The next day, stress-busting deep-tissue massages awaited us at The Spa, which has a refreshingly sensible list of choices ranging from the traditional Swedish massage to the more newfangled treatments like the chamomile body glow or the popular aromatherapy massage.

To round out our trip we read, dozed, and sipped a drink by the Riviera-style swimming pool and then went for a swim. After all, what would a trip to Beverly Hills be without some poolside pampering?

Even if you're not a movie star, after a weekend at the Regent Beverly Wilshire on Rodeo Drive, you'll sure feel like one.

Catalina Island

The Inn on Mt. Ada

398 Wrigley Road
Avalon, CA 90704
Telephone: 310-510-2030
Reservations: 800-608-7669
www.catalina.com/mtada

Highlights

- Exquisite 1920s Georgian Colonial mansion, impeccably restored and maintained

- Mobil Four-Star, *Andrew Harper's Hideaway Report* Award-winning inn

- Ideal site for weddings, honeymoons, and corporate retreats

- Room rate includes: a full breakfast, an ample deli-style lunch, appetizers, fresh fruit, freshly baked cookies, soft drinks, beers, wines, and champagne

- Complimentary use of golf cart for exploring the village of Avalon and surrounding area

- No mobility-impaired accommodations

- Rates from $300 to $640, double occupancy. You can also reserve the entire estate for your wedding party or special event.

Twenty-six miles across the sea, there's an enchanting island called Santa Catalina. The isle has been a favorite vacation destination for Southern Californians for more than a century and was the home of Native American Indians for more than 7,000 years. The main village, Avalon, was founded as a resort town in 1887, with the bantam seaside settlement of Two Harbors approximately an hour's drive away.

William Wrigley purchased the island in 1919, and two years later built an opulent Georgian Federalist Colonial home as a present for his wife, Ada. In addition to his chewing-gum empire, Wrigley owned the Chicago Cubs, and

INN ON MT. ADA EXTERIOR

Catalina became the team's spring training home for 30 years. The Wrigleys typically spent only six to eight weeks per year on the island (coinciding with spring training). In 1975, the Wrigley Family Trust deeded 86 percent of the island to the Santa Catalina Island Conservancy, a nonprofit environmental preservation foundation.

Today, the venerable Wrigley Mansion is known as the Inn on Mt. Ada, but the baronial five-acre estate still evokes a powerful sense of things refined, cultured and sublime—from the time when William and Ada Wrigley held court here from the 1920s until William Wrigley's death in 1932. During their tenure on the mount, the Wrigleys welcomed Hollywood stars, luminaries, and dignitaries such as Presidents Warren Harding and Calvin Coolidge as well as the Prince of Wales. Ada continued to periodically stay at the residence until 1947. Following her death in 1958, the home was opened for tours until the mid-1970s when it was utilized by the University of Southern California as a conference center, and subsequently leased to a private group that presently operates the Inn on Mt. Ada.

The hardwood floors still glisten, the white painted trim and crown molding shines brilliantly. The palatial living room and parlor are surrounded

49

by ample wood-trimmed picture windows while French doors lead to a grand patio with dramatic overlooks of the village and sea. It was the awesome vistas and magnificent sunrises and sunsets over the Pacific that enticed Wrigley to build the mansion for his wife on the mountaintop.

There are six guestrooms, all located on the second floor, accessed via a gracefully curving staircase with intricate balusters and detailing (the home is replete with its original elegant elevator, but for safety concerns is inoperative). Each room varies in size and is uniquely furnished with richly appointed fabrics, paintings, and vintage mosaic-tiles on the bathroom floors and antique furnishings. The Grand Suite features a fireplace, living room, private deck, full bath, and harbor view. The Queen's Aviary also has a fireplace, sitting room, full bath, and harbor view. Windsor Room is a corner abode with fireplace, full bath, harbor and ocean views. Bethany Glen offers a bedroom with dressing area, fireplace, full-bath, and ocean view. Morning Glory is outfitted with a bedroom, dressing area, three-quarter bath, and ocean view. Garden Porch is compact, yet cute as a bug with a full bath and ocean view. The home was designed with every special amenity that one would expect to find in a fine estate: butler's pantry, maids' quarters, formal library, grand piano, salon, sun lounge, club room, and more.

The entire inn is frequently reserved for weddings, private functions, and small corporate retreats (up to 16 guests). Special niceties at the inn include use of a golf cart for explorations around Avalon (auto use is strictly limited on the island and there are no rental cars), wine and cheese, hors d'oeuvres, full breakfast, and a deli lunch are included in your stay.

If your vacation sensibilities tend toward an intimate, refined, and genteel experience, with all of the requisite romantic ingredients, then the Inn on Mt. Ada is the proper place to stay when you visit Santa Catalina.

Zane Grey Pueblo Hotel

Avalon, CA 90704
Santa Catalina, Island
Telephone: 310-510-0966
www.zanegreypueblohotel.com

Highlights

♦ Built in 1926, Western author Zane Grey's former private estate retains its enchanting traditional Hopi-Indian Pueblo architectural character

♦ Honest, unpretentious simplicity—a rustic environment, alive with a spiritual calm

♦ Sixteen rooms (seven ocean view, nine mountain-facing), each named after a Zane Grey novel

♦ Complimentary continental breakfast includes coffee, tea, toast, and whole fruit (coffee and tea available 24 hours)

♦ A library of Zane Grey's books

♦ Each room has a queen and two twin beds, refrigerator and microwave, newly placed rattan furniture. No phones, clocks, or TVs. Bathrooms are utilitarian.

♦ Arrowhead-shaped outdoor heated pool, and superb vistas of village and harbor

♦ Free shuttle service available, walking distance to the village of Avalon

♦ Not recommended for mobility-impaired travelers

♦ Rates from $59 to $175. Summer season (June 1 to mid October): from $135 to $175. Quiet Season (mid October–Mid June): from $80 to $110. Winter Special: Monday through Thursday November 1 to March 31 (excluding holidays) all rooms $59, except Tonto Rim $75 (excluding holidays)

ZANE GREY PUEBLO HOTEL VIEW

A stroll through the understated pueblo perched high on the hillside above Avalon Harbor shimmers with the sense that Zane Grey might still be in his study working on another novel. Not much has been changed over the years around Zane's former domain and his study remains much as he left it. Built in 1926, the architectural style is vintage Southwestern Hopi-Pueblo in style and detail; thick plaster walls, heavy timber beams, ancient weatherworn Saltillo tiles and multi-pane wood-sash windows etched with the patina of touch from decades of use.

The guestrooms are furnished much as one would expect to find in a friend's country guest house. Pure function and utilitarian purpose dictates the Southwest interior motif. The inn is refreshingly honest, inviting, and homey, and all of the guestroom soft goods and furnishings have recently been upgraded. The welcoming sense of being in a home away from home is one of the Pueblo's dominant allures. The living room is striking with its large white-plaster fireplace, hand-hewn timber beam ceiling, grand piano, games, books, and yes, a TV. Equally enticing is the adjacent outdoor patio with wondrous cliff-edge views of the village and harbor.

Zane Grey, the author of more than 89 books and 100 movies based on his works, had this to say about Catalina and his affinity for life at his pueblo: "It is an environment that means enchantment to me. Sea and mountain! Breeze and roar of surf! Music of birds! Solitude and tranquility! A place for rest, dream, peace, sleep. I could write here and be at peace …."

Zane Grey's legacy to Catalina Island includes more than his pueblo. When Hollywood filmed his classic Western saga, *The Vanishing American* on the island in 1924 (more than 300 movies have been filmed on Catalina, including *Treasure Island* and *Mutiny on the Bounty*), the production company imported fourteen buffalo. At the conclusion of filming, the producers left the buffalo behind. Today, there are an estimated 400 wild American "Zane Grey" buffalo roaming Catalina's back country.

The rates are affordable, but the simple quietude and honest energy experienced at Zane Grey's Pueblo are priceless. If you are seeking a refined and polished place, Zane Grey's isn't for you. But if you enjoy monasteries, rustic retreats, and unfettered travel experiences, you will find the Zane Grey Pueblo an intriguing and appealing hideaway.

Avalon from the Zane Grey Pueblo Hotel

Santa Barbara Region

Ojai Valley Inn & Spa

Country Club Road
Ojai, CA 93023
Telephone: 805-646-9622
Reservations: 800-422-OJAI (6524)
www.ojairesort.com

Highlights

- Golf, tennis, horseback riding, swimming pools, whirlpools, and health facilities

- Preeminent 31,000 square-foot spa

- Four-star resort in idyllic mountain setting

- Three distinctive restaurants, poolside snack bar, bar/lounge, pub

- Exceptional outdoor adventures: hiking, biking, kayaking, and fishing

- Children's program

- Handicapped accessible

- Rates from $299 to $2,500. Spa Ojai: No charge to hotel guests, $35 day rate for non-hotel guests or $20 when booking a treatment. Treatments range from $35 to $310

All of the elements were in perfect harmony when I arrived in the Ojai Valley Inn & Spa. It was a warm and sultry afternoon in late August. A lazy breeze wafted gently across the valley. The sun was setting and a pink glow radiated from the craggy mountainsides across the valley. Eucalyptus and oak leaves rustled melodically like Nature's wind chimes. Film director Frank Capra was so smitten by the tranquility and beauty of Ojai Valley that he used the locale as the exterior setting for the mythical land of Shangri-La in the 1937 film-classic *Lost Horizon.*

OJAI VALLEY

The Ojai Valley Inn has been an integral part of Ojai since the early 1920s. Pasadena architect Wallace Neff designed an adobe hacienda with whitewashed plaster walls, massive, hand-hewn timber trusses and red saltillo floor tiles. Neff's timeless creation exemplifies the essence of classic California Mission-revival architecture.

Back in the 1930s and 1940s, the Ojai Valley Inn was the hot place to go for rest and relaxation. Many Hollywood celebrities, including Irene Dunn, Clark Gable, Walt Disney, and Lana Turner were frequent guests.

To recapture its place as one of finest destinations in the West, the Crown family spent more than $35 million renovating the 220-acre resort in 1986, followed by another recent multi-million-dollar renovation. The 1920s-vintage golf course was revamped and realigned under the direction of architect Jay Morrish. With two 200-yard par threes and five 400-yard par fours, Ojai is once again revered as one of the West's premier courses.

In January 1998, the Inn opened a beautiful $10 million, 31,000-square-foot spa that resembles a Moroccan palace. There are 28 treatment areas at Spa Ojai, including massage rooms (five with fireplaces), wet treatment rooms with wall fountains, whirlpools, steam rooms, saunas, and sun bathing loggias. Two very private massage rooms for couples can be booked for several hours or more. Spa services include massage and facials as well as

57

yoga, exercise, and meditation classes. A pool, whirlpools, spa cuisine, and a gift shop add to the ambiance. Without a doubt, Spa Ojai is one of the finest spas on the West Coast.

Activity facilities at the Ojai Valley Inn include eight tennis courts, two heated swimming pools, a gym, and horseback trail-rides. Everything at the Ojai Valley Inn is top-flight, including the cuisine. Sunday brunch at the Inn regularly attracts guests from Los Angeles and Santa Barbara.

Most of the 206 guest rooms and suites are located in the newer buildings. The old-style suites in the 1920s-vintage clubhouse are my personal favorite, with plaster walls, hardwood floors, and original hand-painted Spanish tiles. All accommodations feature fine furnishings, plush carpets, original artworks by local painters, and fully stocked mini bars. In addition, you'll find terry cloth robes, an array of soaps and shampoos, and more towels than you'll ever use. Fifteen of the suites feature parlors and fireplaces.

Once you've been pampered at the Inn at Ojai you'll know for sure that Shangri-La really does exist.

TABLE FOR TWO AT THE OJAI VALLEY INN & SPA

Four Seasons Biltmore
at Santa Barbara

1260 Channel Drive
Santa Barbara, CA 93108
Telephone: 805-969-2261
Reservations: 800-332-3442
www.fourseasons.com\santabarbara

Highlights

- Santa Barbara's premier resort, Mobil Four-Star and AAA Four-Diamond

- Ranked among the top 50 hotels in the world by *Travel & Leisure* magazine

- Central Coast's best Sunday Brunch

- La Marina consistently ranked among Santa Barbara's top three restaurants

- Exquisite garden grounds, ideal wedding site

- Outstanding Mission style architecture, two palatial swimming pools

- 10,000 square-foot spa with extensive cardio equipment

- Exquisite waterfront art-deco style Coral Casino

- 213 rooms, suites and cottages, handicapped accessible rooms and facilities

- Rates from $500 to $3,500. Inquire about seasonal packages.

What's so special about the Biltmore? Just about everything—the architecture is stunning, the flora and fauna are breathtaking, the seaside setting is pure romance, the cuisine is to die for, and the service is impeccable. Any other questions?

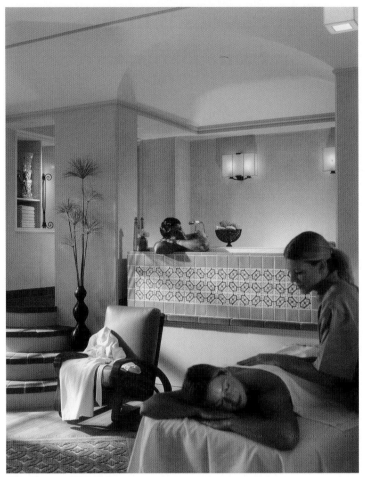

FOUR SEASONS MASSAGE

Slightly intimidated by the Biltmore's reputation as a place of refuge for Hollywood stars and captains of corporate mega-industries, my experience turned out to be disarming and satiated with solace. As I shut off the engine, a valet glided up, opened the car door and cordially enunciated, "Welcome to the Biltmore! Are you checking in?" Before I knew it, my car and luggage were whisked away.

After settling in my room, I returned to read and relax in La Sala lounge. Afternoon high tea was being served, but I was preoccupied with the room's voluminous wood ceiling. It's a masterful network of heavy wooden trusses and formidable, interconnecting hip, valley and jack rafter beams, corbels, knee braces and heavy wrought iron straps and bolts.

All the guest quarters are cozy and enticing. Most of the rooms and suites have balconies or decks, ceiling fans, marble-lined baths, fireplaces, and vaulted ceilings.

The Biltmore's fine-dining venue, La Marina, has maintained a coveted consistency of sophistication for many years, in cuisine and staff, from executive chef to waiter and host. Specializing in American regional cuisine, the chef proclaims with pride, "I don't have to go looking across the country for product. The natural foods grown in the fields locally, combined with the seafood available off the Santa Barbara coast makes menu planning a treat."

The newly expanded and renovated Biltmore Spa and adjoining pool offers guests a state-of-the-art 10,000 square-foot fitness center. The extensive array of equipment and services includes 12 treatment and massage rooms, cardiovascular fitness equipment, a steam room, sauna, and two outdoor whirlpools. Massage treatments are also available in the privacy of your guest room.

As you can imagine, an overnight stay at the Biltmore, like most of the finer things in life, doesn't come cheap. The Biltmore averages close to 100 percent occupancy most weekends of the year, but midweek, Sunday through Thursday nights, you will find a selection of enticing packages that offer a variety of added amenities.

In the mood for romance? Try the Biltmore's Romance Package that includes a two night, three-day stay with a welcome bottle of champagne and an elegant dinner for two overlooking the Pacific Ocean in La Marina. The Biltmore also offers a Spa and Wine Country package.

Simpson House Inn

121 East Arrellaga Street
Santa Barbara, CA 93101
Telephone: 805-963-7067
Reservations: 800-676-1280
www.simpsonhouseinn.com

Highlights

♦ Registered historic landmark

♦ AAA Five-Diamond location

♦ Occupies one acre of lushly landscaped grounds with fountains and mature trees

♦ Main house with six rooms and a restored circa-1876 carriage house with three detached cottages and four suites

♦ Exquisite full breakfast offering vegetarian selections and fresh, organic juices.

♦ Bicycles, English lawn croquet, and beach equipment available

♦ One handicapped-accessible room

♦ Rates from $235 to $450 (including full breakfast and afternoon wine and cheese)

If you're contemplating opening your own bed and breakfast, it is strongly suggested that you first make a pilgrimage to the Simpson House and take good notes. Linda and Glyn Davies purchased the property back in 1975. The one-time Victorian estate had degenerated and this prime commercial property was for sale. The house, considered a major liability, was slated for imminent destruction.

Glyn and Linda didn't know what they wanted to do with the property, but they did know they had to save the old structure. "For a while, we contemplated converting the house into apartments," they recall. In the

SIMPSON HOUSE FOUNTAIN

meantime, they raised their family in the house. When their kids left for college, the Davies transformed the home into an inn, opening the rooms to the public in 1985. The Davies are still actively involved in running the inn, which, because of their vision, retained a distinct sense of home. Thanks to the Davies, the inn's guests enjoy the fruits of 18 years of restoration and foresight.

During the restoration, the main house was extensively remodeled, the Carriage House entirely dismantled, and three new cottages set discretely throughout the existing flower gardens. A quick glance at any of the guest rooms shows that the cost of materials and labor was not an issue. For example, in the upstairs guest rooms, authentic Victorian reproduction wallpaper, imported from England, graces the ceilings and walls. In one room alone, the intricate wallpaper consists of more than 500 hand-cut pieces that cost in excess of $5,000. Everywhere I looked, there was ample evidence of extravagance, from the fancy New England soaps and shampoos to the elegant brass lamps illuminating exterior walkways. The fine linen, china, and glassware awaiting guests at the breakfast table also contributed to the distinct sense of elegance.

Room accommodations range from the efficiently sized Mary Simpson Room, with lace accents, antique bed, and detached bath to the enchanting cottages—Abbywood, Greenwich, and Plumstead—all offering fireplaces, love seats, and lofts. Glyn and Linda blended the new cottages with the surrounding environment so masterfully that one would assume the buildings had been there for decades.

Our upstairs suite in the Carriage House featured a steep-pitched, rough-plank ceiling with exposed collar ties. The exterior walls were ancient, white-washed barn siding. To recreate the exact character of the original carriage house, Glyn had gone to considerable expense by entirely reconstructing the old carriage house, board by board, within the exterior of an entirely new structural shell.

All of the suites and cottages feature private decks or garden patios where you can relax, meditate, and even have your breakfast. Guests are also offered breakfast in the dining room, on linen-draped tables on the veranda, and in the garden. At the Simpson House, the first meal of the day is a gourmet affair, with three courses delivered to your table by the resident innkeeper and her attentive staff. Culinary creations include fresh strawberry crepes, apple French toast, delicious baked pears, homemade granola, fresh organic juices, and coffee.

When we reluctantly packed and departed, we drove out the long driveway, past the tall iron gate and sandstone retaining wall, and turned down Arrellaga Street. I noticed that the one-acre Simpson House was all but hidden from the street by a giant, eight-foot-tall hedge running alongside the street. That seemed so appropriate, considering the Simpson House Inn is the best kept secret in downtown Santa Barbara.

The Hotel Upham

1404 De la Vina Street
Santa Barbara, CA 93101
Telephone: 805-962-0058
Reservations: 800-727-0876
www.uphamhotel.com

Highlights

♦ Oldest continuously operating hotel in Southern California, Circa-1871, remodeled in 2004

♦ One-acre garden grounds with elegant Victorian-era main building

♦ Complimentary gourmet continental breakfast buffet

♦ On-site Louie's Restaurant offers fresh seafood, pasta and California cuisine

♦ Conference facilities for up to 70 people

♦ All rooms are decorated with period furnishings and antiques. Several units also feature fireplaces, master suite Jacuzzi tubs, wet bars, private patios and porches

♦ Just two blocks from downtown State Street's shops and restaurants and a mile from the beach

♦ No handicapped accessibility

♦ Rates from $185 to $295; Garden Fireplace Cottages $295; Suites from $255 to $420

The living room in the main house and the gardens and cottages out back—those are the elements that I unfailingly envision whenever I recall my stay at the Upham. Oh yes, and then there's the broad, covered veranda with its creaky wood-plank flooring, and ornate gingerbread woodwork on the columns and eave supports. And then, there's the vintage, wide stairway, with

THE HOTEL UPHAM

its walnut and mahogany newel post and white painted balusters, leading to the upstairs guestrooms. The mahogany banister is silky smooth and glistens from more than one hundred and thirty years of hands gripping and sliding along its surface.

All of the venerable guest accommodations have been extensively remodeled and updated without removing or spoiling the original details and characteristics that define this wonderful place as truly historic. The original five guest rooms upstairs, the cottages built during the 1920s and the newer units as well, are all furnished with designer-quality furnishings and antiques. Paintings and prints on the walls, down comforters on the beds, little accent pieces thoughtfully placed here and there, even the plush carpeting, all these touches and more perpetuate the orchestrated efforts by the owner and interior designers to create a warm and friendly home-like environment.

Everything about the Upham reaffirms the flavor of being in a home or a small country inn. Another reason why the property exhibits an intimate atmosphere is due to the mature vegetation. A canopy of stately shade trees and colorful floral-gardens soften the presence of the cottages and the carriage house to the rear of the property.

In addition to the appealing guest accommodations, the Upham shines best in its public spaces. The living room, with luxurious stuffed couches, side chairs, and fireplaces, serves as the perfect room for visiting and relaxing. The inner courtyard-gardens beg for one to come sit in a lawn chair and relax with a book or to just shift the mind into neutral and do absolutely nothing. The ability to feel just as comfortable and at ease when you are outside of the confines of your room is an essential ingredient that is often lacking at corporate style hotels, but it is sure one of the Upham's most disarming distinctions.

Today, the neighborhood is graced with towering palms, pines, and giant deciduous trees. But back in 1873 when the inn opened for business, there was an unobstructed view all the way to the wharf. Local legend says that the widow's walk served as an important aid for the chef. When a sailing vessel was scheduled to arrive in Santa Barbara, he would send an assistant down to the wharf with a set of signal flags. From the widow's walk, another assistant would peer through a telescope and await a semaphore message from his dockside companion, indicating how many departing passengers were en route to the inn, and the chef could then plan his meals and place settings accordingly.

THE HOTEL UPHAM LOBBY

El Encanto Hotel and Garden Villas

1900 Lasuen Road
Santa Barbara, CA 93103
Telephone: 805-687-5000
1-800-346-7039 (CA only)
www.elencantohotel.com

Highlights

♦ A ten-acre Garden of Eden snuggled on a hillside high above the city

♦ Mobil Three-Stars location; Charter member, Historic Hotels of America. Member, Orient Express Hotels

♦ Impressive Spanish Colonial Revival and Craftsman bungalow cottages in a tropical garden setting

♦ Outstanding restaurant with *al fresco*, terrace dining offers dramatic city and harbor views

♦ Five-star wedding venue

♦ Swimming pool, tennis courts with on-site pro, Sandpiper Golf Course located nearby

♦ Concierge, sitter service, complimentary valet, multilingual staff

♦ Seven handicapped-accessible accommodations

♦ Rates from $269 to $759

If Santa Barbara was a dominion, then surely the King and Queen's castle would be situated on the hillside site of present day El Encanto Hotel. From its mountainside perch, the El Encanto commands an encompassing view of the Santa Barbara Mission, the city, and the harbor. If the view was all the El Encanto had to offer its guests, the journey there would still be worth the time and effort. Set on ten tropical garden acres, with a wealth of hibiscus, bougainvillea, banana trees, giant bird of paradise, palms,

EL ENCANTO HOTEL AND GARDEN VILLAS

pines, and eucalyptus, the resort is one of Santa Barbara's architectural and environmental treasures. El Encanto is a prime pick for wedding ceremonies, receptions, and honeymoons.

The property was first developed by James Warren in 1916 when he built six cottages for use as student and faculty housing. At the time, the State Normal School—the precursor of the University of California, Santa Barbara—was located across the street. The present-day main lodge was opened as a hotel in 1918. Additional cottages were built during the 1920s and early 1930s to accommodate wealthy, wintertime vacationers from the East Coast and Midwest.

The Spanish-style casitas with red tile roofs and white stucco facades have aged gracefully with the decades. Today, the cottages appear almost as organic outgrowths of the surrounding, lush tropical flora.

In addition to the free-standing one and two-bedroom cottages with fireplaces and incredibly enchanting living rooms, there are also newer, more conventional units that were built in the late 1970s. All 84 guest accommodations feature televisions, Frette linens, duvets, down featherbeds and pillows, two plush terry robes, high-quality designer furnishings, fabrics and artwork as well as natural aloe-based soaps and shampoos in the baths. The rooms are individually decorated and offer mountain, garden, city, or ocean views. Most rooms have fireplaces, hardwood floors, porches, patios or balconies. Every accommodation offers dataport, coffeemaker, iron and ironing board, mini-bar, telephone with voicemail, and a work area.

The El Encanto Dining Room and lounge has been a favorite with Santa Barbara residents for decades. It is a ritual for locals in the know to gather on the outdoor patio for sunset cocktails and dinner. That's when the panoramic view of Santa Barbara is most magnificent. After you have experienced one of the awesome sunsets from the El Encanto's patio, you'll understand exactly why they call the town and hillside *The Riviera*.

*EL ENCANTO HOTEL
TERRACE VIEW*

Bacara Resort & Spa

8301 Hollister Avenue
Santa Barbara, CA 93117
Telephone: 805-968-0100
Reservations: 877-422-4245
www.bacararesort.com

Highlights

♦ 78-acre oceanfront setting on the outskirts of Santa Barbara

♦ Luxury rooms and suites with all the fine touches

♦ 42,000-square-foot spa including a full-time spa concierge

♦ The Spa Café offering healthful coastal cuisine

♦ The Spa Shop stocked with workout gear, make-up, and skin-care products

♦ 3,500-square-foot cardio and weight studio offering one-on-one training

♦ On-site dining and entertainment venues

♦ Handicapped accessible

♦ Rates: $395 for Garden View rooms; $950 and up for Junior Suites; and $2,500 for a stay in the Penthouse Suite (call for rates on the palatial Presidential Residence)

There is a place where California's chaparral-dotted mountains fuse with the cobalt Pacific with such other-worldly beauty that for thousands of years Native Americans referred to it as "Anacapa," or "the mirage."

Better known today as the American Riviera, the coastal enclave of Santa Barbara blends history, romance, sheer physical beauty, and sophistication with dazzling results. But nowhere is the essence of Anacapa better epitomized than at the recently opened Bacara Resort.

BACARA FITNESS TRAIL

Bacara is an indulgent seaside refuge on the outskirts of Santa Barbara. This new member of the elite California coastal resorts has deftly positioned itself as the creme-de-la-creme of world-class spa resorts. Bacara melds fine cuisine and wine with sumptuous accommodations and rejuvenating spa experiences. Bacara is all about golden days, glossy nights, play, sea, sky, sun, golf, the good life, the right stuff, pamper and polish, wine and dine, see and be seen.

Bacara is situated on 78 picture perfect oceanfront acres, dappled with oaks and eucalyptus trees, nestled along two miles of sandy beach. The luxurious resort pays Gatsby-esque homage to the glamour of old Hollywood through its Mission-style architecture and first-class service—fine-tuned to please its "discriminating and demanding clientele."

All of the 311 luxury rooms and 49 specialty suites offer tranquil views, in-room spa services, 24-hour room service, top-notch bath delights, mini bars, high-speed Internet access, and video entertainment systems. Half of the units also feature fireplaces. Amenities on the grounds include more than 25,000 square feet of social and meeting space, a conference center, and a screening theater that seats over 200 people.

There are ample options for imbibing, including the Lobby Lounge and Director's Lounge, the Bacara Bar, and the upper-level Rotunda with panoramic vistas. Miro is Bacara's fine dining venue, situated on a bluff above the Pacific. The Bistro, a pleasing alternative, is geared toward relaxed, casual dining and specializes in Mediterranean cuisine.

The nearby 1,076-acre Ranch at Bacara, a working avocado and lemon ranch, supplies the resort's organic herbs and vegetables and provides guests with a tranquil setting for such outdoor activities as hiking, mountain biking, and horseback riding.

Many Bacara guests come specifically for its famous and accommodating spa. The 42,000-square-foot facility offers a full-time concierge and such signature treatments as the citrus-avocado body scrub, oatmeal-sage body polish, and crystal sea therapy. The spa also offers hydrotherapy; ayurveda; several types of facial treatments; and a complete array of hair, nail, and waxing services.

When the urge to nibble strikes, the Spa Café serves healthful coastal cuisine. For bath and beauty products, visit the Spa Shop, which is stocked with workout gear and make-up, as well as Kiehl's, Phytomer, and Tara skin-care products. Additionally, for those who love to exercise even when on vacation, the 3,500-square-foot cardio and weight studio offers one-on-one training.

Whether you come for the spa, the food, or just the glamour, you won't be disappointed. With all the amenities Bacara has to offer, this world-class spa resort promises to pamper, polish, and rejuvenate you.

Bacara Resort Courtyard

The Ballard Inn

2436 Baseline Avenue
Ballard, CA 93463
Telephone: 805-688-7770
Reservations: 800-638-2466
www.ballardinn.com

Highlights

♦ Named one of the "Top Ten Most Romantic Inns" by *Historic Inns*

♦ AAA Four-Diamond resort since 1994

♦ Intriguing antiques and understated Western-flavor interior design

♦ Tranquil, rural setting in tiny village of Ballard

♦ Savory, complete gourmet breakfast included in rate

♦ Afternoon wine tasting and hors d'oeuvres

♦ Popular with honeymooners

♦ Theatre, wine tasting, golf, nature hikes, art galleries, shopping nearby

♦ Three handicapped-accessible rooms

♦ Rates from $215 to $305

As you stroll up the rustic gravel path past the white picket fence and neatly manicured garden and onto the inviting wraparound porch, you begin to suspect that your stay at The Ballard Inn will be a romantic one. The multiple stone chimneys and clapboard dormers effuse country charm and warmth. Once inside, you discover that each of the 15 uniquely designed rooms reflect the characteristics and history of the Santa Ynez Valley. Each dormer window looks out onto the tiny, enchanting town of Ballard.

We stayed in Cynthia's Room, which honors one of early Ballard's most important characters, Cynthia Ballard Lewis. Cynthia married the town's founder, George Lewis, who named the village after William Ballard—his

THE BALLARD INN

good friend and Cynthia's first husband. (On his deathbed, Ballard asked his wife to marry Lewis.)

Cynthia's airy room pays homage to love and friendship, with its double wedding-ring quilt, portraits of Cynthia's two husbands, white marble and emerald velvet antique appointments and white brick fireplace, above which hangs a portrait of Cynthia herself.

The Davy Brown room is a classic. You can relax in a rustic mountain-man's chair as you watch the flames flicker in the primitive native-stone fireplace. Two of the interior walls are made of hand-adzed dark wood logs complete with cement chinking between each course of timber.

The Fiesta room recalls the days of fandangos and fiestas during California's Spanish Colonial days. An intricately detailed ceremonial sombrero hangs proudly above the fireplace mantle. Period pictures on the walls recall the days of Ranchos and Spanish Land Grants, while antique chairs set in front of a large multi-pane window face an elegant green "fainting sofa."

Jarado's room is decorated in tribute to the Chumash Indian assistant to William Ballard. You'll find feather-trimmed baskets, arrowheads, even a tomahawk, while the color motif of red, white, and black is taken from the Chumash cave paintings found in the area. Other rooms include: The

Western, The Vineyard, The Green, El Alamo Pintado, The Mill, Lyon's, Windmill, Mountain, Equestrian, and the Wildflower. The Vintner's Room and the Stagecoach Room are comfortable meeting rooms that make a perfect small retreat, corporate or otherwise.

Special in-room touches include a complimentary welcome basket of chocolate, cheese, fruit, and crackers and the Ballard Inn's unique bath amenities that include wine soap, wine hand lotion, and champagne shampoo. Additional amenities include wine tasting certificates for local wineries, homemade cookies at bed turndown, bottles of San Pellegrino sparkling water, and fragrant herbal soaps, lotion and shampoo suitable for both men and women.

Each afternoon the Inn offers a complimentary wine and hors d'oeuvres tasting, which is served in the Vintner's room. There were seven excellent local wines served the day we came, including vintages from Curtis, Firestone, Kalyra, Prosperity, and Santa Barbara Winery.

Dinner is served at the Inn's own Café Chardonnay every Wednesday through Sunday from 6:00 to 9:00. Its main dishes run $16 to $25. The Café's atmosphere is made intimate with candlelight and lanterns. During colder months, the enormous Italian marble fireplace warms the restaurant and lobby with its glow.

The master of the kitchen is an accomplished chef whose signature dishes attract locals from all over the Santa Ynez Valley. The menu features local produce, and includes fresh fish, meat, and vegetarian offerings. The wine list is two pages long, and almost exclusively local. Desserts include selections for chocolate addicts and calorie counters.

Most people come away from the Ballard Inn raving about the exquisite breakfasts served in the William Ballard dining room. In addition to an array of fresh fruits, juices, coffees, granola and more served buffet style from a sideboard, there's also a full menu of breakfast meals prepared by gourmet chefs.

More than the food, the location, or the antiques in every room, what makes The Ballard Inn a special place to stay are the people who run it. The staff is more than just friendly and helpful—they professionally anticipate the needs of the guests.

Guests are left to themselves and given ample opportunities for privacy and quiet. There are no televisions in the rooms, so couples can relax into the comforts, light the fireplace, and enjoy the warmth of unique surroundings and the smile of a loved one.

The San Ysidro Ranch
& Stonehouse Restaurant

900 San Ysidro Lane
Montecito, CA 93108
Telephone: 805-969-5046
Reservations: 800-368-6788
www.sansysidroranch.com

Highlights

♦ One of the world's foremost wedding and honeymoon destinations

♦ 38 accommodations in 21 diverse storybook cottages, swimming pool, two tennis courts, and horseback riding nearby

♦ Over 500-acre estate with extensive trail system for hiking

♦ Delicious dining at ultra-romantic Stonehouse Restaurant and Plow & Angel Bistro

♦ King-size beds with Frette linen and goose-down comforters, wood burning fireplaces, and hot tubs

♦ En-suite spa treatments include massage and facials

♦ Member Relais et Chateaux

♦ One fully handicapped-accessible unit, one partially

♦ Rates from $399 to $4,100

The San Ysidro Ranch is a captivating resort. When travelers return from a stay at the Ranch, they inevitably describe their experience with reverence and a look of contentment that lets you know that they'd love nothing more than to immediately return for another dose of indulgence.

The lobby has all the classic attributes of a well-maintained farmhouse, but a small sign clearly indicated that it was the office. Inside, the overstuffed couches, oak plank floors, and multi-pane wood windows enhance a comfortable sense of home.

SAN YSIDRO LIVING ROOM

The Ranch is set on more than 500-acres with 38 accommodations in 21 separate cottages. A maze of connecting pathways wend, Hobbit-style, from cottage to cottage through meandering gardens.

If Vivian Leigh or Jackie "O" could come back for a reprise visit today, they would surely indulge in a spa treatment, or two, or three. San Ysidro's Body Works spa services—en suite, by reservation—include Swedish, Pre-Natal, Deep Tissue, Esalen, Children's Massage, Shiatsu, Craniosacral, Thai, and Sports massage.

For decades, local Santa Barbarans have made the San Ysidro Ranch's fine dining facilities a first choice for special occasions from pre-wedding rehearsal dinners to anniversaries, as well as a favorite destination when out of town friends come to visit. The American Regional cuisine relies on locally grown fresh produce as well as on-site organic garden-grown herbs, vegetables, and fruits. The rustic, open-beam ceilinged Stonehouse Restaurant is an off-the-charts destination for romantic candle-lit dining. The gracious staff share their exceptional knowledge of regional wines and food and wine pairing.

Every room and cottage accommodation offers king-size beds, Frette linen, goose-down comforters, distinctly-elegant furnishings, soft-goods and amenities throughout; the difference is primarily in size and added touches such as fireplaces, dining rooms, living rooms, and private decks with hot tubs.

For an ultra-romantic stay at the Ranch, request the Kennedy Cottage—John and Jacqueline's West Coast honeymoon abode back in 1953. This seductively charming little manse, with a winsome hand-hewn stone façade, is tucked in a foliage-shrouded secluded corner of the property, and yet it's a short stroll to fine dining in the Stonehouse Restaurant. Highlights include two bedrooms, three fireplaces, the largest private deck of all units, two bathrooms, and a separate living room.

Equally inspiring is the 2,200 square-foot Eucalyptus Cottage, graced with two bedrooms, two-and-a-half baths, three fireplaces, spacious dining room, and dining area. Added amenities include a full complimentary bar, a very private ten-meter swimming pool, and hot tub.

Inside, the three-room Rose Suite was well seasoned but spotlessly maintained. Its freshly buffed oak floors dipped and angled slightly. French doors and wood windows further enhanced the feeling of a charming bygone era.

In any room, a stay at San Ysidro Ranch will have you feeling mellow, relaxed, and indulged.

GARDEN AT SAN YSIDRO

The Alisal

1054 Alisal Road
Solvang, CA 93463
Telephone: 805-688-6411
Reservations: 800-425-4725
www.alisal.com

Highlights

- 36 large studios with wood-burning fireplaces and twin beds

- 37 two-room suites with king or twin beds, sitting room and fireplace

- Private bungalows with large front verandas, three bedrooms, two baths, spacious living rooms and fireplaces

- Modified American Plan—includes breakfast and dinner

- Trail rides, golf (two 18-hole championship courses), tennis, swimming, hiking, bicycling, fishing, canoeing, kayaking, and boating

- Handicapped accessible rooms and facilities

- Rates from $485 to $550 double; includes breakfast and dinner

The Alisal, California's premier guest ranch, is just 45 minutes from Santa Barbara and only a mile and a half away from the Danish-style village of Solvang. Surrounded by the rugged Santa Ynez Mountains, the ranch is snuggled in a narrow, oak and sycamore-laced valley.

As I turned off the county road and drove down the Alisal's private drive, I was instantly tranquilized by the pastoral vision of three motionless horses standing on a nearby hilltop, silhouetted by the setting sun. The aroma of fresh-cut hay wafted through the air. The muffled sounds of horses whinnying drifted from the barns. Birds peeped and cawed from the treetops, while a distant farm tractor growled in a perfect baritone in accompaniment to the Alisal's symphonic sounds of nature.

THE ALISAL TRAIL RIDES

Soon, a most interesting thing occurred. My inner clock went into slow motion. Everything was so hushed and serene that I found myself subconsciously searching for some noise, some chatter, or at least the din of a television set. I realized that the absence of televisions and telephones in the guest rooms is a necessary step toward spiritual and physical rejuvenation, part of the reason why people come to the Alisal.

The Western ranch-style guest cottages are unpretentious, with furnishings that are rustic, sturdy, and simple. The Alisal features two 18-hole championship golf courses, seven tennis courts, a large heated pool, and a 96-acre private lake that is stocked with a variety of boats and, of course, fish.

A few employees have been with the Alisal since 1946 when the dude ranch first opened. Wranglers and waitresses alike talk of interacting with the children and grandchildren of guests who first came to the Alisal as kids themselves years before.

For the duration of your stay at the Alisal, a specific dining table is reserved in your name. Several entrées are offered each evening, as well as a special fish, vegetarian dish, salad, and soup of the day. At breakfast, you can order off the menu or help yourself to a buffet of fresh fruits, pastries, granola, and other treats.

A romantic and adventurous alternative to the traditional morning meal is the fabled "breakfast trail ride." Guests meet their cowboy escorts at the barns around 7:30 A.M. for an hour-long ride to a historic adobe in the hills above the Ranch. Riders are greeted with fresh coffee, hot chocolate, and Danish pastries served in front of a campfire while the cowpokes cook up a memorable ranch-style breakfast of sausage, flapjacks, bacon, and eggs. If you're a late riser, you can still catch a two-hour-long afternoon trail ride. Offered on a daily basis, there are rides designed for the beginner, intermediate, and advanced equestrian.

People adore the Alisal for a variety of reasons—some for the quietude and isolation, others for the abundance of activity options. One woman confided, "The Alisal is really a summer camp for adults—even though our kids think the place was created just for them."

THE ALISAL
GUEST ROOM

Central Coast

The Seaventure Hotel

100 Ocean View Avenue
Pismo Beach, CA 93449
Telephone: 805-773-4994
Reservations: 1-800-662-5545
www.seaventure.com

Highlights

♦ Excellent beachfront setting, steps from Pismo Pier and seaside shops

♦ Mobil Three-Star and AAA Three-Diamond resort

♦ Award-winning restaurant, Tapas bar, room service

♦ Full array of massage services and body treatments

♦ Four-star quality decor and amenities

♦ Private balcony hot tubs on ocean and mountain facing decks

♦ Inquire about seasonal and mid-week specials that include a Golf Getaway, low priced Hideaway Package, Romance Package, and popular Honeymoon package

♦ Three handicapped-accessible rooms

♦ Rates from $129 to $179 for a mountain-view room with fireplace; $239 to $349 for partial to full ocean-view with king size feather bed, fireplace, and private balcony spa

An ideal vacation destination, the Seaventure is located front-row center on the beach (one of only two true oceanfront resorts on the entire Central Coast) and in the heart of town. It is also a perfect home-base for exploring the village and shops of Pismo, walking along the seashore, strolling on the pier, joining an early morning fishing expedition, kayaking, cruising on peddle surreys, playing beach volleyball, taking sunset walks, surfing, or doing absolutely nothing at all.

SEAVENTURE DECK AND HOT TUB

The resort is set on a wide sandy beach, but the rooms are so enticing that one is tempted not leave them. There is a generous use of rich green and pink marble throughout the hotel. The character of the guest rooms is a perfect balance of feminine and masculine touches. The bedspreads, linens and towels are first quality, while the accent colors, with a sophisticated use of dark forest greens and soft pastels, harmonize pleasantly with the adjacent sand and sea.

All of the interior furnishings, such as the Cape Cod-style white picket headboards and armoir/TV cabinets, were designed by the owners and constructed on-site by craftsmen. Upscale in-room amenities include cable TV, three telephones with data ports, clock radios, coffee makers, and an extensive array of personal items such as soaps and shampoos. All guest rooms are designated no smoking. Every room has a gas-log fireplace, wet bar, and refrigerator. All ocean and mountain-view room are outfitted with hot tubs on private starlit decks. The Seaventure also offers a complete array of spa services including, circulatory, lymphatic, deep tissue, and sports massage.

If you're in pursuit of unadulterated romance, be sure to inquire about the three-bedroom Beach House. It's a free-standing pole structure, smack dab on the beach and a harmless short stroll from Seaventure proper. Equipped with a full kitchen, hot tub, and enclosed deck, the Beach House is ideally suited for honeymooners and wedding parties as well as executive retreats and family reunions.

The hotel's restaurant is one of the Central Coast's most popular dining spots and the Sunday Brunch is commonly regarded as "The Best on the Central Coast." Located on the third floor, the restaurant offers panoramic views of the sea, wharf, and coastline. Morning, noon, or moonlit night, the view is always spectacular. The Tapas bar, adjoining the restaurant, offers mixed drinks and a wide range of appetizers. This venue is equally popular with locals as it is with hotel guests.

The Seaventure menu offers a wide array of dishes, and naturally, fresh-caught seafood from the Pacific is a house specialty.

The Seaventure is a prime oceanfront destination recommended for any occasion, from an anniversary or honeymoon to a long overdue weekend getaway.

The Apple Farm Inn

2015 Monterey Street
San Luis Obispo, CA 93401
Telephone: 805-544-2040
Reservatons: 800-374-3705
www.applefarm.com

Highlights

- Excellent wedding and reception facilities, popular honeymoon destination

- AAA Four-Diamond resort

- Swimming pool and Jacuzzi

- Traditional American meals served in a country ranch setting, on site pastry chef creates daily assortment of cakes, pies, muffins, and more

- Expansive gift shop

- Three handicapped-accessible guest accommodations

- Rates from $119 to $209 off season, weekdays; $139 to $329 weekends in summer

Bill and Katherine Brunk, business travelers from Konawa, Oklahoma, have this to say about their Apple Farm experience, "There are more sophisticated hotels in the world, but you'll have a hard time finding a place that beats the Apple Farm's attentive service and attention to detail." And from the moment you step foot on the property, there's ample evidence of Apple Farm's obsessive quest for perfection.

Flower gardens and plantings look like a fleet of gardeners manicured them only moments previously. The Victorian-style buildings are all in pristine condition—no peeling paint, no signs of wear and tear. Step into the main lobby and you'll be greeted with a friendly smile from a cheerful desk clerk. Katherine Brunk also notes that, "Every single employee who

The Apple Farm mill

we interacted with exhibited a warm and refreshing generosity of spirit. We also really appreciated the free carafe of coffee delivered to our room in the morning."

A fastidious sort, Katherine said that her room was so spotlessly clean that she poked her head under the bed, "just out of curiosity—to see if there were any dust bunnies that the maids might have missed. I peered under the bed and was greeted by a discretely-placed card with the printed words, 'Yes, we clean under here, too!' " Katherine recalls with a chuckle.

All around are numerous examples of an almost fanatical quest for perfection in the details. There's a circular stairway that ascends from the lobby to the second-floor guest quarters—a grand staircase, with turned-oak balusters, that's frequently used as a backdrop for group wedding photos. On-site Apple Farm venues for private parties and wedding receptions include the Garden Room and Quilt Room. Additionally, the Mill House Terrace, highlighted by towering white birch and water perpetually cascading off the mill wheel, is unbeatable for its enchanting sense of rural tranquility.

Each of the Inn's 70 guest rooms features a four-poster bed (some with a canopy), a gas-log fireplace with mantle, custom-crafted bleached pine furnishings, and oversized baths. Extensive use of crown molding and other wood trim work are in evidence throughout the property. And every room has its own identity—no two are alike. Each one abounds with fine early-American country furnishings, including a bedside porcelain lamp with a hand-painted deco-band of lacy flowers—the lamp's deco-band being an exact custom-crafted replica of that room's unique wallpaper motif.

A red painted wooden apple with a golden stem and leaf, the symbol of the Apple Farm, is set on a counter in every guest room. The manager explains, "We give the apples to each guest as a remembrance of their stay. We have one woman who stays here often—she proudly says that she has a bowl at home containing, at last count, 53 apples. We thought about putting the Apple Farm logo on them, but the apples serve as wonderful conversation pieces just as they are."

THE APPLE FARM
GUEST ROOM

Without a doubt, the most romantic Apple Farm accommodations are hidden away, upstairs in the shingle-sided Millhouse. There are only two suites in the Mill House, but that's okay—it makes these rooms all the more special. The Mill House (as well as some Trellis Court accommodations) also feature hot-tub spas on private decks. One suite is decorated with white rattan furnishings, white walls with blue accents, and lots of artwork. The other suite, with rich dark greens and dark oak trim, is the more masculine of the two. Both suites have outside, private decks—one overlooks San Luis Creek while the other has views of the pool and the water-wheel flume. If you're looking for a honeymoon or anniversary getaway spot, the Millhouse suites are highly recommended. And to complement the celebration, a complete array of body treatments is also offered at the Apple Farm's Spa. Services include Swedish, deep tissue, aromatherapy massages, body scrubs, exfoliation, seaweed wraps, and foot and hand treatments.

Apple Farm's restaurant is well known for its specialty—traditional American meals served in a country ranch setting. Ask someone who has experienced an Apple Farm meal and they're bound to respond with loving recollections of hot apple dumplings, fresh baked cornbread with honey butter, fruit cobblers, homemade soups, and apple pie à la mode.

On a historical note, not many places offer the chance to see a working gristmill. But down by the old millstream, adjacent to San Luis Creek, Leo the millwright carefully adjusts the water flow through the flume then engages the main drive shaft of the 14-foot-tall, three-ton water wheel. Leo points to the main hub and Babbitt bearings and says with pride, "Some of these parts are from a 150 year-old mill in Cold Springs, New York. The bearings, from Indiana, are more than 100 years old. As long as we continue to keep them well oiled, I imagine they'll last another 100 years or so." Leo quickly steps inside the millhouse, with the impish grin of someone who truly loves his job, to prepare for another day of apple pressing, ice cream churning, and flour grinding on the stone gristmill.

If Americana intrigues you, consider a stay at the Apple Farm Inn. Mom would approve.

Inn at Morro Bay

Sixty State Park Road
Morro Bay, CA 93442
Telephone: 805-772-5651
Reservations: 800-321-9566
www.innatmorrobay.com

Highlights

♦ Waterfront location with magnificent views of Morro Bay and Morro Rock

♦ Waterfront restaurant and lounge with panoramic bayside vistas

♦ Guest rooms feature high-quality furnishings, many with private spas on private outdoor decks or balcony's, feather beds, and fireplaces

♦ Highly recommended wedding/reception/honeymoon location

♦ 18-hole golf course directly adjacent to property, with a complimentary bucket of range balls

♦ Outdoor heated pool, complimentary mountain bikes, full-service catering

♦ On-site massage services

♦ ADA compliant

♦ Rates from $89 to $309. Inquire about special Wine, Spa, Romance, and Leisure packages

The scene surrounding the Inn at Morro Bay is alive with brawny commercial fishing boats chugging to and from the open sea, moored at anchor, and slumbering at the docks. Herons, gulls, and pelicans soar through the sky and float lazily on the water—paying scant regard to the ducks, otters, and gulls. Sail boats and pleasure craft rock at ease, tied to buoys in mid-bay, while beyond the sandspit, majestic and rugged Morro Rock (known as the

INN AT MORRO BAY GUEST ROOM

Gibraltar of the Pacific) looms like a behemoth silent-sentinel standing guard over the harbor entrance.

If it's a honeymoon or anniversary that brings you to the inn, be sure to request the Bayfront Cottage. Located away from the other guest rooms, this romantic suite almost hangs over the water; you can enjoy the dramatic bay views from a private patio, the oversize sunken tub or outdoor Jacuzzi.

It is no wonder the inn is one of the region's most popular venues for weddings, receptions, and honeymooners. All of the Inn at Morro Bay guestrooms are first-class, with casually elegant accents, fireplaces, beam ceilings, thick terry-cloth robes, and all the amenities of an upscale property.

The rooms are first-rate but it is ultimately the lush gardens and serene seaside vistas that make this a destination of unfettered enchantment. The Inn at Morro Bay is one of those special places that casts a spell over you the moment you drive down the eucalyptus-lined drive and step across the lobby threshold—and you're held comfortably in its seductive grasp for the duration of your stay. The sounds of the breeze rustling through the trees and the barking of seals are the dominant auditory accents—although sometimes the inn's nearest neighbors—a federally protected blue heron rookery—create a real ruckus! (There is also a rare peregrine falcon preserve on Morro Rock. The surrounding area is a veritable birders' paradise.)

Celebrated on-site amenities include a waterfront restaurant, the Orchid, that specializes in fresh, seasonal fair from local farms as well as fresh-caught seafood supplied by local fishermen. The dining room and lounge feature ceiling-to-floor picture window views of the bay and rock. Locals regularly dine here, especially when celebrating a special occasion. A full range of on-site and in-room massage services include circulatory, deep tissue and sports massage. Directly across the street, there's an 18-hole golf course and just a few steps down the eucalyptus-lined road you'll find the informative Morro Bay State Park Museum of Natural History. Within easy walking distance is The Embarcadero, the town's waterfront shopping district. Carmel it is not, but it does offer a wide array of gift shops, shell shops, ice cream parlors, coffee shops, canoe and kayak rentals (whale-watching boats depart regularly from the harbor during migration season), art galleries, and casual, come-as-you-are seafood diners as well as upscale eateries.

INN AT MORRO BAY
LOUNGE AT DUSK

Blue Whale Inn

6736 Moonstone Beach
Cambria, CA 93428
Telephone: 805-927-4647
Reservations: 800-753-9000
www.bluewhale.com

Highlights

♦ Understated elegance

♦ AAA Four-Diamond location

♦ Beautiful ocean setting

♦ Recipient of Arington's "Twenty-Five Best in the Nation" award

♦ Great place for honeymoons and anniversaries

♦ One handicapped-accessible room

♦ Rates from $190 to $250

Located at the northern end of Cambria Village's New Town—in the midst of an irregular line of Moonstone Beach mini-motels, B&Bs, inns, antique shops, restaurants, and homes—rests the Blue Whale Inn. Many of the Moonstone Drive enterprises are set on lots no bigger than a typical residential parcel, which is why most inns offer few guest rooms.

Limited to six suites, the Blue Whale's amenities, personal touches, and elegance are equal to that of a fine resort hotel's. The Inn's common room has an uncommon panoramic picture window. Across the street is a narrow strip of grassy bluff with the ocean perched behind it. If you look carefully along the bluff-top, you might discover a few circular depressions in the sandstone outcroppings—the remnants of prehistoric Chumash Indian food-grinding pestle sites.

BLUE WHALE INN
GARDEN

The Blue Whale Inn provides an exceptional atmosphere for interacting with other guests or for simply relaxing. With a glass of wine in hand, it is tempting to lounge in the living room and watch the sun set over the Pacific as otters cavort and whales swim by during their annual migration between Alaska and Mexico. The furnishings, coordinated wallpapers, and window treatments make the common room, and all of the guest suites, feel refined and inviting.

Faced with the challenge of a long, narrow lot, the architect designed a saw-tooth shaped structure so that every room would have an unobstructed ocean view.

An equally important decision was positioning the parking strip along the opposite property line. Rather than viewing a row of cars directly in front of the rooms, guests look out over a soothing English garden—complete with stone paths, waterways, and meditation benches.

Highlights of the guest suites include English floral-print fabrics, royal-size canopy beds, fireplaces, mini-refrigerators, armoires and love seats, writing desks, and skylights that bathe each room with warmth and light. Extra-large, tiled bathrooms are brightly illuminated by picture windows that overlook the private garden area.

The innkeepers, adept at making guests feel welcomed and at ease, are an essential reason why the Blue Whale is an exceptional place to stay.

Big Sur Region

Post Ranch Inn and
Sierra Mar Restaurant

P.O. Box 219, Highway 1
Big Sur, CA 93920
Telephone: 831-667-2200
Reservations: 800-527-2200
www.postranchinn.com

Highlights

♦ Breathtaking vistas from the edge of the continent

♦ Award-winning Sierra Mar Restaurant

♦ Heated basking and lap pool set on the cliff edge overlooking the Pacific

♦ Gift shop, massage services, yoga, aromatherapy, facials, tarot readings, stargazing talks, and guided nature walks

♦ Children highly discouraged

♦ Handicapped accessible, all guest rooms are non-smoking

♦ Rates from $455 to $835, singles and doubles. Two-night minimum on weekends. Add $100 for each additional guest

Big Sur is one of the world's most spectacular natural regions. What draws people here from all parts of the globe is the intense beauty that is, so far, relatively immune from develpoment. You will encounter a few farms scratched out of the forest, a handful of inns, filling stations, and general provision stores, but hike a few yards off the highway, and the civilized world will suddenly feel a thousand miles away.

The Post Ranch experience is unique. Architect Mickey Muennig designed a cluster of avant-garde structures utilizing basic materials such as redwood, concrete, and rust-tinged metal. Some of the abodes are reminiscent

POST RANCH INN SUNSET

of intertwined redwood water towers, while one unit's roof design mimics a soaring butterfly. Other habitats are partially submerged in the earth with a profusion of wildflowers growing on the sod roofs.

The most dramatic edifice is definitely Sierra Mar, the resort's award-winning, cliff-hanging restaurant. Under the direction of acclaimed restaurateur Tony Perault, Sierra Mar quickly developed a dedicated following among discerning Monterey Peninsula bon vivants and is known as one of only 11 restaurants worldwide to receive the *Wine Spectator's* Grand Award for an outstanding wine list.

The interior of Sierra Mar is specifically crafted to highlight the glorious sunsets and ever-changing daytime extravaganzas performed by the ocean, sky, and mountains. A continuous ribbon of floor-to-ceiling glass panels, framed in slender steel tubing, creates the illusion that the restaurant is hovering in space, a thousand feet above the Pacific.

When you return to your room after dining, you can continue to enjoy the inspiring scenery, as all guest rooms are oriented to maximize ocean, mountain, and celestial views. In-room amenities include wood-burning fireplaces, stereo systems, quality bath products, large Rajah slate Jacuzzi tubs, complimentary beverages and snacks, coffee makers, private decks, and king-size beds with massage table discretely stowed underneath.

There are 30 guest units at Post Ranch: ten coast houses, six units in the whimsical Butterfly House, two mountain houses, five ocean houses, and seven tree houses. All of Meunnig's buildings were designed to minimize their impact on the surrounding environment. The architect went to great lengths to avoid disrupting the existing terrain, and reportedly, only one tree was removed during the construction process.

It's hard to pick a favorite unit, as each one portrays a distinct set of temptations. For example, we stayed in one of the coast houses with a cliff-edge location, a sensational 1,200 feet above the Pacific. At sunset, we relaxed and watched the sun sink far out over the ocean.

I presumed that most everyone would insist upon an ocean view room. But the next morning, as I walked through one of the mountain houses, I discovered a markedly different but equally engaging view of the Ventana Wilderness's towering, craggy peaks.

One of the inn's most attractive qualities has nothing to do with amenities and accommodations. Some of my fondest Post Ranch Inn memories centered around the gracious and intelligent staff members. They were always friendly, offering impeccable service.

The Post Ranch Inn offers solitude not every location can provide. If peace and relaxation in the untouched beauty of nature are what you're looking for, Post Ranch Inn is the perfect getaway spot for you.

POST RANCH INN DUAL MASSAGE

Ventana Inn & Spa

Big Sur, CA 93920
Telephone: 831-667-2331
Reservations: 1-800-628-6500
www.ventanainn.com

Highlights

♦ 243 acre, rustic resort, 1,200 feet above the Pacific

♦ Mobil Four-Star restaurant, cocktail lounge, and gift shop

♦ Continental breakfast with goodies from onsite French bakery

♦ 62 standard rooms to large suites, all with private balconies or patios, some with fireplaces

♦ Japanese hot baths, saunas, two pools, and clothing-optional sun decks

♦ Renowned Allegria Spa at Ventana with a special emphasis on Thalasso therapy, Pelotherapy treatments, and essential oils

♦ Large gift shop and fine art gallery features regional artists

♦ One handicapped accessible room

♦ Rates from $459 to $1,100 for standard and fireplace rooms and suites

Ventana's bluff-top setting in wild and rugged Big Sur, with commanding views of the Pacific ocean and the surrounding Santa Lucia mountains, is an essential reason why this resort is revered as a legendary and a truly world-class resort hideaway. The prestigious *Andrew Harper Hideaway Report* has rated the inn as one of the top ten in the world. Additional accolades and awards include: *Mobil Travel Guide's* Four-Star rating, *Conde Nast Traveler's* Gold List, and *Wine Spectator's* "Award of Excellence." Ventana was also given one of the highest ratings by *Zagat's* survey, 25 on a scale of 30.

Ventana Inn & Spa South Coast View

Surprisingly, a prime Ventana attraction is the absence of "things to do." You won't find a tennis court, putting green, or game room here. Savoring the silence, far from the high-tension cacophony of urban life is the element that most guests cherish at Ventana. As soon as you step from your car in the parking lot, you'll immediately sense Ventana's soothing energies.

The rustic, understated architecture and the interior design of the guest quarters and main lodge deftly pay homage to the surrounding pristine environment. There's a beckoning library with plush seating in the glass and heavy timber-accented main lodge where afternoon wine, cheese, and fresh fruit are served. There's also an outdoor trellised seating area that is a great place to savor the fresh air and soak in the powerful vistas of the Pacific coastline in the near distance.

In addition to the incredible diversity of services offered at the renowned Allegria Spa (strongly recommended to make reservation at least two weeks prior to arrival), the inn's fitness room is replete with Tectrix stationary bicycles, multi-station Nautilus equipment, and free weights.

Ventana's dramatic structures are predominantly pole-frame construction with exterior facades clad in natural, weathered cedar siding. Interiors are graced with heavy timber beams, the walls are finished with aromatic cedar paneling and the furnishings are likewise rustic but elegant. All accommodations are outfitted with TV-VCRs and refrigerators. Some of the rooms feature native-stone fireplaces and saltillo tile floors. The large suites also feature wet-bars, dining alcoves, and outdoor private spa tubs.

You will pay a premium for an ocean view room, but the vistas from the mountain facing rooms are just as spectacular in their own manner. From any room, it's an easy walk down to the pool or the patio of the main lodge. A series of paved trails interconnects the guest cottages, pools, and main lodge. The restaurant is a delightful eighth of a mile walk away, but you can also drive your own car or take Ventana's convenient shuttle.

The Mobil Four-Star rated Cielo restaurant at Ventana specializes in gourmet dishes served California style—fresh, seasonal, and locally produced ingredients. Cielo is a popular dining destination for Carmel and Monterey residents and travelers making the Highway 1 journey as well.

For wedding and special occasions, Ventana is superb with its majestic setting combined with excellent food and service. A private and secluded Lower Terrace is a popular venue for wedding ceremonies. The Upper Terrace is adjacent to Cielo, the restaurant at Ventana.

If you like to hike, the old Coast Ridge Road is easily intercepted just a few yards from the upper swimming pool. The Ridge Road meanders along the craggy Santa Lucia's for more than six miles, revealing spectacular Big Sur vistas.

Those who have previously stayed at Ventana agree that the staff's charming and gracious attitude is exceptional and an important reason why guests return for reprise visits.

If you are planning a weekend or summertime getaway, make reservations at least six months in advance (although, it never hurts to call at the last minute to see if there might be a cancellation).

Ventana was designed and built specifically to offer the finest in service and amenities, the overnight rates are correspondingly impressive—a special haven where the expense is handsomely repaid by the dreamy memories.

Monterey Peninsula

Highlands Inn,
Park Hyatt Carmel

120 Highland Drive
Carmel, California 93923
Telephone: 831 620 1234
Reservations: 800-682-4811
www.highlandsinn.hyatt.com

Highlights

- One- and two-bedroom Spa Suites and Sur units—all with ocean views

- Mobil Four-Star and AAA Four-Diamond resort

- Most accommodations feature fireplaces and full kitchen

- A premier wedding and honeymoon venue for close to a century

- Pacific's Edge Restaurant is *Wine Spectator* magazine's "Grand Award" winner

- California Market for casual dining, indoors and spectacular al fresco patio seating

- Heated pool, jogging trails, outdoor spas

- Five handicapped-accessible units

- Rates from $225 (standard room, garden view) to $385 (deluxe, ocean view); Suites $455. Inquire about seasonal, mid-week specials.

Back in 1917, Californians were raving about the breathtaking beauty of Highlands Inn, Carmel's brand new hideaway resort. During the early planning stages and construction of this remote lodge, locals chastised and laughed at developer J. Franklin Devendorf. They warned him that his frivolous and isolated enterprise was doomed to fail.

Highland Inn Spa Suite

To reach Devendorf's rustic retreat, guests had to make an arduous, all-day ten-mile buggy ride from the Monterey train station. But once they arrived, guests reveled in the energizing beauty of one of the world's most dramatic and exhilarating vistas—the craggy cliffs and rocky shores of the Big Sur coastline.

More than 80 years later, people still speak of the romantic retreat with unabashed words of praise and adoration. The Inn's reputation is so stellar that the legend of this place, like a story passed down through the generations, has grown to extraordinary proportion.

The intensity of the setting is an overwhelming delight to the senses—the forest of rich green, towering Monterey pines perfectly complements the distant sounds of waves slamming against rocks. Faint calls of barking sea lions and birds cawing add a lyrical dimension to the romantic setting. It is inspiring to know that you are witnessing the very same breathtaking scenes and sounds that Jack London, Ansel Adams, Robinson Jeffers, and others delighted in so long ago. The spectacular natural setting is ample reason to come and savor a stay at Highlands Inn.

In recent years, many changes have occurred at this hillside haven. In 1984, Highlands Inn underwent a $40 million renovation. Most of the old cottages were torn down and replaced by new units, although the stunning main lodge still appears much as it did in 1917. The original, exterior yellow-granite facade and the graceful low-slung hip roof of the main lodge were left relatively unchanged but, inside, dramatic transformations and alterations were made. The dark natural-wood interior was made bright and spacious. Walls were plastered and tinted white or soft pastels with light-oak wood accents. Small windows were replaced with extensive glass-panels and mitered-glass corners that span from floor to ceiling. Dramatic, architectural skylights now bathe this stunning lodge and dining room with a dazzling radiance of

HIGHLAND INN DINING

light. An additional renovation in 2003 upgraded rooms furnishings and soft goods, installed new Jacuzzis, and generally polished the property.

The luxurious guest accommodations are scattered around the pine and oak forested hillside property in more than 20, detached shingle-sided and shake-roof structures. Situated on a dramatically terraced hillside, all rooms are fresh, airy and outfitted with first-class amenities. Suites feature full kitchens, hydro-massage baths, spacious dressing rooms, pullout queen-sized beds and priceless views.

Dining at the Highlands is an experience unto itself. The Inn's Pacific Edge Restaurant blends a quintessentially romantic setting with matchless cuisine to produce an impressive list of international awards. It's no wonder it has hosted the Masters of Food and Wine event—a gathering of the most celebrated chefs and winemakers in the world—for nearly two decades. Every menu choice is outstanding.

Fewer than 20 hotels around the world merit the elite Park Hyatt moniker, a mere eight of those in North America. With the Highland's stellar reputation for awesome scenery, beautifully appointed rooms, and highly praised cuisine, discriminating travelers need look no further to find a little slice of the good life.

Stonepine Private Estate

150 East Carmel Valley Road
Carmel Valley, CA 93924
Telephone: 831-659-2245
www.stonepinecalifornia.com

Highlights

♦ California's oldest thoroughbred horse farm

♦ Complimentary Monterey Airport pickup with limousine

♦ Classical French-style gardens for the perfect wedding location

♦ Croquet field, exercise room, and heated pool

♦ Suites bearing the names of different designers, decorated with exquisite antiques

♦ Comprehensive equestrian center with sulky track, hunter-jumper course, arena, and trail offering romantic hay rides

♦ Sixteen suites, all with Jacuzzi tubs, large sitting areas, CD/DVD players, terry cloth robes, and Brown & Jordan bath amenities

♦ French chef de cuisine offers daily menu and champagne reception nightly

♦ Spa massage services available in the privacy of your room

♦ Yoga, tai chi, and power walks with private instructor

♦ No handicapped accessibility

♦ Rates from $275 to $1,250. No children under 12. Includes full breakfast. Inquire about special packages offered throughout the year.

STONEPINE PRIVATE ESTATE LAKE VIEW

This magnificent California resort retreat was originally built in 1930 as the private residence of Henry Potter Russell and Helen Crocker. Double H Ranch soon became known as California's first and foremost thoroughbred horse farm. To perpetuate the estate's southern European atmosphere, Mrs. Russell planted Italian stone pine seedlings around the perimeter of the house. Today, the stone pines average 80 feet in height.

Double H Ranch remained in the Russell family until Noel and Gordon Hentschel purchased the property in 1983 for use as a private horse ranch.

The Hentschels embarked on an ambitious and costly renovation of the property. Before long, the Chateau, surrounding gardens, and equestrian center were once again the talk of the town. Stonepine opened its doors to the outside world in 1986.

The Stonepine experience begins at the impressive wrought iron gate just off Carmel Valley Road. The mile-long driveway leads you across a small bridge that spans the boulder-strewn Carmel River and past white triple-rail fences, thoroughbred horses grazing in the fields beyond. The narrow, paved road weaves in and out of dark forests of California live oaks. Onward, the journey continues across the newly planted Stonepine vineyard. Before the first glimpse of the Chateau comes into view, you'll pass by English hunter-jumper training arenas; a two-story, semi-circular horse barn and equestrian center; and a polo field and sulky track.

In the foyer, you'll find elegant, high ceilings and a seventeenth-century stone French fireplace. Clearly, no expense was spared in creating this home fit for royalty.

The grand living room overlooks the formal gardens and original Romanesque swimming pool and is a truly sublime sight to behold. Out on the loggia, accessed through French doors off the living room, there are hand-carved stone columns.

One of my favorite features at Stonepine is the circular, tile-roofed tower. It houses my very favorite room at the chateau, which is appropriately accessed through a secret passageway. The tower comes as a bonus when you rent the 1,050-square-foot Taittinger Suite at $900 a night. Taittinger's royal amenities include separate his and hers baths and changing rooms, a marble Roman-style Jacuzzi, fireplace, and king-size bed.

For $600 a night, you can occupy the Don Quixote Suite. This lovely accommodation features Spanish motifs, his and hers baths, a sitting room with fireplace, French doors leading to a private rose garden, and a secret door that leads from the master bedroom to the chateau's library.

If you're suffering sticker shock from the princely sums mentioned so far, there are less baronial accommodations that are relative bargains. For example, rooms in the Paddock House at the nearby Equestrian Center range from $275 for Lady Bolero to $550 for the Russell Suite.

For pure romance, lovebirds often request the two bedroom, $750 per night Briar Rose Cottage. Equipped with its own dining room, kitchen, entertainment room, and private bar, Briar Rose is set apart in a forest not too far from the main house.

The newest addition is the incredibly comfortable and luxurious Hermes House, with two bedrooms, living room, dining room, and kitchen, plus exercise equipment and an outdoor private patio, all for $1,250 per night.

Once you've entered Stonepine's gates, you will experience a level of comfort that will transport you to new heights of luxury. Breathe it all in: if you are at Stonepine, it's because you've earned it.

Bernardus Lodge

Post Office Box 80
415 Carmel Valley Road
Carmel Valley CA 93924
Telephone: 831-658-3400
Reservations: 888-648-9463
www.bernardus.com

Highlights

◆ Tranquil rural setting surrounded by pines, oaks, vineyards, and towering mountains

◆ Enchanting rustic architecture radiates sense and scale of home

◆ The 57 guest rooms (525 to 1,872 square-feet)

◆ Amenities and services include a wine and cheese greeting upon arrival, in-room complimentary wine and gourmet snack pantries, fresh fruit and flowers

◆ Spa services include romantic couples room and outdoor private therapy pool. The Salon offers full array of services

◆ Resort and Marinus Restaurant awarded Mobil Four-Stars and coveted *Wine Spectator* Grand Award for maintaining one of the world's foremost wine lists

◆ Four handicapped-accessible rooms

◆ Rates from $475 to $750; suites from $1,115 to $1,730. Be sure to inquire about seasonal packages.

In the study of architecture, there's a term "value added by design." In the case of Bernardus, it's "Exceptional value added by top-flight service, sophisticated amenities, idyllic setting, and award-winning cuisine."

The difference is in the details at Bernardus. From the fine cuisine to the luxuriant guestrooms there's a consistency of architecture, design, and panache throughout the property.

<small>BERNARDUS LODGE LIVING ROOM</small>

The tranquil, rural setting surrounded by Monterey pines, stately California live oaks, vineyards, and towering Santa Lucia Mountains harmonizes soothingly with the rustic and yet dynamic design elements. From the moment you're escorted through the entryway, a powerful sense of serenity and architectural honesty pervades the senses. Huge timber beams, weathered but glistening pecan wood plank flooring, rich ochre plaster-walls and French doors with a dramatic radius window above deftly frames an outdoor trellised courtyard and the hillside beyond.

The guestrooms are exceptional, with lavishly comfy featherbeds, Italian linens, Carmel Valley limestone-framed fireplaces, French doors opening onto decks or patios, and elegant oversized baths with two-person tubs and separate showers. The distinguished guestroom character is enhanced through the use of overstuffed sofas and chairs, antique amoires, dark polished-woods and vaulted ceilings. Every five-star touch, such as cableTV, CD player, hair dryer, in-room safe, robes, iron and ironing board are discretely tucked at the ready in your room.

One of the first things I noticed upon entering our room was two bottles of wine, an amply stocked pantry full of gourmet snacks, aromatic fresh-cut flowers, a bowl of fresh fruit, a tea service, and coffee maker. I presumed that the tempting amenities (like the proverbial mini-bar) came with a heavy surcharge, but I was impressed when the valet mentioned that the coveted items were all complimentary. The gratis in-room amenities serve as a perfect metaphor for the gracious Bernardus experience.

Amenities and services at the Spa at Bernardus Lodge include the romantic Vineyard Room designed for couples, complete with oversized shower and outdoor private therapy pool. In addition to eight treatment rooms, a "warming room," exercise room, sauna, Vichy shower, steam rooms, and a beauty salon, there is also an outdoor warming pool and a tranquilizing meditation garden.

The Salon utilizes locally found flowers and herbs as well as essential oils and healing waters in the spa treatments.

Ancillary spa services include acupuncture sessions, personal fitness training, therapeutic stretch, one-on-one meditation, tennis instruction, yoga, croquet, and bocce lessons.

Bernardus has firmly established its reputation as a wedding venue and naturally offers complete bridal beauty services. To maintain its discrete atmosphere, the Lodge limits wedding ceremonies and parties to one per day.

The Bernardus dining experience is superlative. Marinus, the fine dining venue, specializes in California contemporary cuisine, while Wickets Bistro offers equally enticing fare in a casual, club-like atmosphere and al fresco dining. Of course, room service and poolside dining are also available. If you are a fan of the culinary arts, inquire about the Chefs Table dining in the main kitchen of Marinus. Accommodating up to six diners, you'll have a front row view of the stove and line work area of the bustling kitchen.

Bernardus cuisine features organic herbs and produce grown onsite in a two-acre garden, as well as a special herb garden adjacent to the restaurant's outdoor terrace.

For a more intimate experience, inquire about dining in the resort's elegant wine cellar (maximum eight diners).

Signature dishes at Marinus include seared Monterey Bay Spot prawns served on a bed of crispy vegetables with a black truffle vinaigrette and an Alder Smoked Sonoma Duck prepared grilled, served atop a pastilla, adorned with turnip puree and spice bread jus.

All the way around, from the people to the rooms and the fine cuisine and wine—Bernardus is an outstanding destination that's mighty hard to leave and perpetually beckons you back for a reprise visit.

Quail Lodge

8205 Valley Greens Drive
Carmel, California 93923-9515
Telephone: 831-624-2888
Reservations: 888-828-8787
www.quaillodge.com

Highlights

- Tranquil setting on 250 acres in sunny Carmel Valley

- Mobil Four-Star Award

- 18-hole golf course, swimming pool, spa, tennis courts

- 83 luxury guestrooms and 14 sumptuous suites

- On-site award winning The Covey restaurant

- Ideal site for weddings, banquets, and corporate functions

- New wellness center and complete luxury spa services

- Leading Hotels of the World

- Four handicapped-accessible rooms

- Rates from $225 to $825

Quail Lodge's facilities are understated, with rustic wood exteriors of coffee brown and interiors favoring earth tones. The suites are open with high ceilings and well supplied with the finest amenities. Of the 97 units, four are Executive Villas, which provide guests with an expansive living space and a private garden area with jacuzzi. Newly installed interior design elements in the rooms and suites include Roman shades, cozy window seats, overstuffed cushions, and upholstery. The fresh color palette mirrors the outdoor environment through ample use of mossy greens, rich red, and earth tone colors. Hemlock-wood floors, copper sinks, wrought-iron sconces, and

QUAIL LODGE EDGARS PATIO

boar-hide leather completes the welcoming warmth of the residential/familial luxury accommodations.

The new Wellness Center, located within the Clubhouse, offers trend-setting therapies such as nutritional counseling and analysis, blood testing, and metabolism studies. It also features an outdoor yoga garden and fitness center. The spa, located at the Resort, offers three outdoor treatment room cabanas, four indoor treatment rooms, a Jacuzzi and pool, pedicure/manicure facilities, hydrotherapy, steam, and Vichy showers.

Quail Lodge's commitment to serenity is shown in many ways. At most first class resorts, guests are pampered—but at Quail Lodge there is a level of service that is truly remarkable. Staff members describe how wonderful it is to work at the Lodge, and how well the staff is respected by management, and how this translates into one of the warmest, down-home experiences in the midst of Carmel's well known opulence. As a guest, I felt like royalty and family at the same time!

Like many Carmel-area resorts, golf is a main attraction at the Lodge. The course is short, 6,521 from the back tees. In other words, it is not an intimidating monster of a course. It is, however, a delight to the senses, and is made challenging by the strategic placement of ten lakes along the generally flat terrain following the old riverbed of the Carmel River.

Besides golf, the Quail Lodge also offers tennis (three hard surface courts), hiking, biking, and swimming, as well as assistance to guests who desire to explore the Monterey Peninsula.

Although there are many fine dining opportunities around Monterey, guests at Quail Lodge need only book reservations at the resort's award-winning restaurant, The Covey, for one of the most memorable meals of a lifetime. The chef de cuisine has developed a menu that blends traditional favorites (the Covey Rack of Lamb is superb) with more adventurous flavors. The chef explores new flavors to go with the wealth of fresh vegetables and fruits (often grown locally at organic farms) and fresh fish from Monterey Bay (the locally "farmed" abalone is divine).

Quail Lodge has earned its legendary reputation through its commitment to service and excellence. Check-in and check out the Carmel Valley in all its glory.

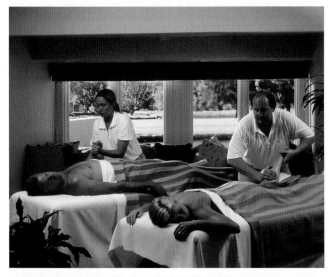

QUAIL LODGE
DUAL MASSAGE

La Playa Hotel

Corner of 8th & Camino Real
Carmel-by-the-sea, CA 93921
Telephone: 831-624-6476
Reservations: 800-582-8900
www.laplayahotel.com

Highlights

♦ Historic circa–1904 Mediterranean style hotel

♦ 75 rooms and suites, plus five distinguished cottages

♦ Four-star wedding/reception locale

♦ Steps from the beach and downtown shops

♦ On-site gourmet restaurant, full-service catering

♦ Swimming pool, bicycles, free parking

♦ Member: Historic Hotels of America—a program of the National Trust for Historic Preservation

♦ Three handicapped-accessible rooms

♦ Rates from $175 to $295; suites and cottages from $335 to $675 per night. Inquire about midweek and off-season specials.

La Playa is one of those places that has been hosting, quite nicely thank you, for almost a century. Some guests who first stayed at La Playa as children on summer vacation with their parents now return with their own children or grandchildren. Others who were married or honeymooned at La Playa come back to recall and renew their bonds of love and refresh cherished memories.

A fine blend of ingredients attracts people to La Playa—it's located in the heart of Carmel and it's a short, two-block stroll to the beach. The hotel is so close to the sea that if you keep your bedroom windows open at night, the

La Playa dining

mesmerizing sounds of crashing waves and the muted call of seals, gulls, and sea lions are bound to sooth your soul.

La Playa's award-winning gardens contain more than 3,500 plants, including a spectrum of flowering perennials and exotic roses as well as deciduous and evergreen trees. This spectacular outdoor environment is an important reason why the resort has become one of Carmel and California's foremost wedding sites. On weekends, during the spring marrying season, the hotel often hosts two weddings a day, one in the morning and another in the afternoon.

Because most of the guest rooms were built back in the 1920s when small guest rooms were the norm, the standard guest quarters are not nearly as spacious as those found at contemporary properties (La Playa also offers larger mini-suites). Many of the rooms have ocean views—for which you'll pay a premium—while others overlook the gardens or the town. The rooms are painted a luminous white and they all have sizable windows with plantation shutters, so even though they are compact they are never the less compelling and comfortable.

Breakfast, lunch, dinner, and an outstanding Sunday Brunch are served in the Terrace Grill—specializing in creative California-cuisine presented in a casual environment. Al fresco dining doesn't get much better than a candlelit dinner on the Grill's open-air terrace with its tranquil vistas of village and sea. The adjacent rich wood-paneled lounge offers full cocktail and bar service. Poolside dining and bar service is also offered.

La Playa's best kept secret is its five romantic cottages, discretely nestled among sprawling oaks, Monterey pines, cypress, and a profusion of colorful annual and perennial plantings. The cottages are conveniently located a half block from the hotel. All are eminent examples of the snug storybook cottages that abound throughout Carmel. Every cottage features fireplaces, patios, terraces, wet bars, and full kitchens.

My favorite is Loghaven Cottage. As its name implies it is an authentic, rustic log cabin. A two-story stick frame, Craftsman-style addition was added to the rear of the three bedroom cottage some years ago. Upstairs in the addition there's a large master suite with two double beds, a bathroom, and a sitting area with a queen hide-a-bed. Downstairs there are two bedrooms

La Playa Hotel

and one and half baths, a full kitchen, dining room, and living room—both with fireplaces.

Tradewinds Cottage is a two-bedroom, two-bathroom unit with fireplace and kitchen that is ideal for two couples or families of up to six people. Moongate Cottage is a spacious one bedroom with fireplace and a hide-a-bed in the living room, kitchen and a private patio. Homeport Cottage offers the same amenities as Moongate. Skyway Cottage, a favorite with honeymooners, is a secluded 1 bedroom with a large wet-bar and refrigerator, a hide-a-bed, and outdoor terrace.

La Playa Hotel was a favorite hideaway for travelers long before Carmel was recognized as a world-class vacation destination. The resort hotel was first a private estate designed and built for noted California artist Christopher Jorgensen's bride, a member of San Francisco's Ghirardelli chocolate family. When the Jorgensens moved into their villa in 1904, the palatial residence was one of Carmel's most impressive homes, complete with the town's first swimming pool.

Artists, writers, and influential friends from San Francisco and Carmel were invited to the Jorgensen's estate for lavish dinner parties. Sadly, seven years later, Mrs. Jorgensen died. Shortly thereafter, Mr. Jorgensen leased the home to a Mrs. Signor, and moved away, never to return to the home he lovingly designed for his wife. Mrs. Signor added 20 rooms and converted the mansion to a hotel. In the mid-1920s, an ailing Mrs. Signor relinquished the managerial reigns to her two sons, Harrison and Fred Godwin.

Shortly after taking over, a fire gutted much of the original structure, spurring the Godwins to add 30 rooms. La Playa's reputation spread and vacationers came from far away for extended summertime vacations at the resort. Stays of a month or more were quite common in those days, and rates averaged $5 a week. In 1940, another 30 rooms were added as well as a spectacular ocean view restaurant built at a cost of $80,000. When the Cope family, the present owners, purchased La Playa in 1983, it was much overdue for structural and cosmetic renovations. The property was closed for an eight month, $5 million remodel that included structural modifications, the addition of fine European antiques from the Cope's family collection, and complete conference facilities for up to 150 people.

When La Playa, the town's second oldest hotel, reopened in 1984, it reclaimed its title as Carmel's foremost historic resort hotel.

The Monterey Hotel

406 Alvarado Street
Monterey CA 93940
Telephone: 831-375-3184
Reservations: 800-727-0960
www.woodsidehotels.com

Highlights

♦ Beautifully restored circa-1904 downtown boutique hotel

♦ AAA Three-Diamond resort

♦ Two block walk to Fisherman's Wharf

♦ Located in the heart of Monterey's historic district

♦ Elegant furnishings and finishes

♦ No handicapped accessibility

♦ Rates from $139 to $189; Junior Suite $219, Fireplace Suite $299. Inquire about mid-week and off season specials

The three story, turn-of-the-twentieth-century Monterey Hotel, adorned with brick and terra cotta trim and elegant circular bay windows, is the discreet grand-dame of downtown Monterey.

While wandering down Alvarado Street, I caught a glimpse of the front entry—an inconspicuous, narrow entry-corridor leading to a beveled glass door with an adjacent, simple brass plaque inscribed, "The Monterey Hotel."

The modest entry belies the intricate detailing inside the post-Victorian hotel. I was most impressed by the plaster pillars, complex column cornices, pressed-panel ceilings, and the vintage Otis elevator—Monterey County's first.

With a two-story atrium, theater-style gallery railings, cozy accommodations, and friendly staff, the hotel is reminiscent of an intimate, European pensión.

Monterey Hotel

The lobby and common areas are graced with evocative, impressionistic paintings of Monterey, Carmel, and Cannery Row.

The guest rooms are outfitted with custom armoires, original artworks, and four-poster beds with down coverlets. The standard rooms are small, in the fashion typical of early twentieth-century hotels. The large master-suites, equipped with private fireplaces and spa-tubs, have commanding views of Monterey's harbor.

A delicious continental breakfast served buffet style in a downstairs common room includes juices, coffee and tea, seasonal fresh fruits, fresh home-style baked breads, and pastries. Wine, tea, cheese, and crackers are served in the lobby every afternoon and evening. A popular destination for corporate retreats and meetings, the hotel is located one block from the Monterey Conference Center and has its own dedicated conference facilities, as well.

Hotel Pacific

300 Pacific St.
Monterey CA, 93940.
Telephone: 831-373-5700
Reservations: 800-554-5542
www.hotelpacific.com

Highlights

♦ Design and decor reflects old Monterey and Southwest motifs

♦ AAA Four-Diamond resort

♦ Excellent expanded continental buffet breakfast and afternoon tea service

♦ Two outdoor spas located in garden courtyards

♦ Six handicapped-accessible rooms

♦ Rates from $189 to $349

While strolling along Pacific Street in Monterey, I discovered the Hotel Pacific just a few weeks after it opened for business. I was instantly attracted by the seductive beauty of the main building that recalls the most engaging qualities of a grand California Mission-revival home from the1930s. As I stepped inside the lobby, I was enthralled by the high, rough-timber ceiling and supporting hand-hewn trusses. Sunlight beaming in through a ridge-top skylight illuminated the terra cotta tile floor and the interior plaster walls. I was most impressed by the structure's ageless appearance. The surface textures and hand-adzed timbers suggested the historic, 200-plus-year-old adobes that are found throughout the surrounding neighborhood.

To enhance the hotel's relationship with the gentrified neighborhood, the architects specified wood shingle roofing rather than the more traditional Mexican clay tiles—as Spanish and Mexican Colonial-period Monterey homes were all originally roofed with wood shingles.

A five-foot-wide, saltillo tile stairway leads graciously from the lobby to a broad interior balcony. To the rear of the balcony, a pair of French doors opens to an ample but intimate living room that is enriched by a large fireplace surrounded by stucco walls and hearth. Bookshelves on either side of the fireplace help guests feel at home in a storybook hacienda.

The melded Monterey-Southwest design motifs continue unabated throughout the property. Outdoor gardens in secluded inner courtyards with umbrella-shaded rustic picnic tables offer sedate places to read and relax while listening to the soothing sounds of water cascading from wall-mounted terra-cotta fountains.

The guest rooms carry the hotel's charismatic motifs as well—interior walls are finished with a hand-applied texture, while the floors are hardwood and bleached oak, accented with area rugs in the living and dining areas, with carpeting in the bedroom areas for warm toes. We enjoyed the southwestern-style four-poster feather bed with an overstuffed down comforter. Saltillo tiles grace the bathroom floors, the tub surround as well as shower walls. There's also a clay pot on the vanity brim full of luxury bath amenities. All rooms and suites also feature mini-bars and complimentary coffee and apple cider.

Stepping through plantation-style shuttered French doors, I chose our private deck as my favorite spot for relaxing and unwinding. I watched fishing boats chug in from the open ocean and gazed at the crescent-shaped shoreline that arcs so gracefully up the coast, past Moss Landing, all the way to Santa Cruz.

Hotel Pacific breakfast

126

I was so smitten by the enchanting Hotel Pacific that I inquired with the concierge about the visionary behind the interior's exquisitely picked and placed furnishings and accents. She informed me that the renowned hotel designer Charles Gruwell was responsible for the work. I immediately called Gruwell and we met in the hotel's patio the following morning. He confirmed my presumptions about the hotel's design philosophy. "We utilized elements from local historical structures and blended in Southwestern motifs." He added that pouring through *Architectural Digest* issues from the early 1930s provided many inspiring ideas.

With a new taste of old Monterey, Hotel Pacific offers a handsome and romantic getaway any time of year.

Hotel Pacific patio

Spindrift Inn

652 Cannery Row
Monterey CA 93940
Telephone: 831-646-8900
Reservations: 800-841-1879
www.spindriftinn.com

Highlights

♦ Five stars for romance

♦ AAA Four-Diamond and Mobil Three-Star resort

♦ Aquarium and special packages

♦ 42 rooms, nightly turndown service with Swiss chocolates, silver tray continental breakfast delivered to your room, morning newspaper, afternoon wine and cheese

♦ Two handicapped-accessible rooms

♦ Rates from $199 to $429 per night, double occupancy. Inquire about off-season special packages.

As soon as I settled in my room I cracked open a window to listen to the surf. It was nighttime and a low covering of clouds hung above the bay. I sat on the window seat and watched the waves and heard a drumming on the windowpanes. It took me a moment to realize the sound was from raindrops splattering on the glass. A minute later the rain became a torrent and then the night sky lit up white from a bolt of lightening, followed by the crack of thunder. Welcome to majestic Monterey, Spindrift Inn style.

If you're looking for a place to stay in Monterey, and you just want a warm, well-lighted place, don't stay at the Spindrift. But, if you're in the mood for romance and indulgence, then by all means make a date with Cannery Row's most elegant waterfront inn.

SPINDRIFT INN EXTERIOR

A broad selection of restaurants, nightclubs, and wine tasting boutiques are just steps from the inn. A historic merry-go-round is directly across the street and the Monterey Aquarium and the Tin Cannery Outlet shopping complex are only two blocks down the street. Aside from the neighborhood appeal, the pampering makes the Spindrift Inn special. When you arrive in the afternoon, there's a spread of cheese, crackers and other nibble-items and a selection of regional wines awaiting in the lobby/living room area.

With exquisite oriental carpets, antiques, and a wood burning fireplace, the lobby is bathed in sunlight, filtered through a glass skylight four stories up, during the day (it's even more romantic at night). The best of the Spindrift is without a doubt the oceanfront rooms. There are street-side abobes as well, but if you're going to make the journey, why not go all the way? Guest rooms feature upholstered window seats and king-size canopy beds with plush goose down-comforters. Other highlights include polished oak floors, marble baths, upscale soaps and toiletries, cozy waffle-weave robes, nightly turn-down service, CD players, a writing desk, and a sitting area in front of a real wood-burning fireplace with logs ready to light. The multi-pane, casement windows overlooking McAbee Beach and Monterey Bay are most enchanting.

The continental breakfast in bed for two, delivered on a silver platter to the room in the morning, reaffirmed my thoughts about the Spindrift's romantic qualities.

In the neighborhood, lingering evidence of John Steinbeck's *Cannery Row* is still here for the observant—there's the old Wing Chong Market (Lee Chong in Steinbeck's book), Flora Woods' Lone Star café and house of ill-repute (now functioning as Mackerel Jack's Trading Company). A half block down the street from the aquarium you'll find the site of the Pacific Biological Laboratories, operated by Steinbeck's close friend, Edward F. "Doc" Ricketts. The ramshackle, waterfront lab is presently closed to the public but hopefully the city or a historical society will eventually open it as a public museum. Look closely and you'll discover more Steinbeck treasures lingering around Cannery Row.

Spindrift Inn view

The Inn at 213 Seventeen Mile Drive

213 Seventeen Mile Drive
Pacific Grove CA 93950
Telephone: 831-642-9514
Reservations: 800-526-5666
www.innat17.com

Highlights

- Completely charming, classic 1920s Craftsman residence
- 14 rooms in Main house and two detached structures
- Vistas of Monterey Bay and tranquil garden grounds
- Spacious rooms with all the comforts of a fine hotel
- Jacuzzi under the stars
- Short stroll to village of Pacific Grove, museums, restaurants, golf, Point Pinos Lighthouse, and seashore
- Gourmet breakfast, evening wine and hors d'oeuvres
- One ADA handicapped-accessible room
- Rates from $145 to $240

Inviting is an understatement. Set far back from the street, a wrought iron fence with brick pilasters frames a broad lawn with a flowered perimeter. The property, and the surrounding neighborhood, is blessed with an abundance of towering eucalyptus, oaks, and redwoods that accentuate the greenery with dapples of shade and light. The enchanting two-story white clapboard-sided façade with multi-pane wood sash, accented in forest green, tantalizingly beckons you to step inside and make yourself at home, and that's just what we did.

THE INN AT 213 SEVENTEEN MILE DRIVE

The interior is equally seductive with its rich natural woodwork and high wainscot paneling. A massive stone fireplace and wicker settees underscore the bright and cheerful living room. Common spaces and guestrooms are bestowed with intriguing original works of art, period antiques, and Native American artifacts.

With a view of either Monterey Bay or the gardens, every guest room is outfitted with fresh flowers, antique and period furnishings, TVs and telephones, chocolates, down comforters, private baths, terry robes, and non-allergenic soaps and creams.

Each room, named after indigenous feathered-friends, offers a singular flair and motif. Commodious Blue Heron is striking with its oriental rugs, bay views, and French doors opening onto a balcony with garden overlooks. In addition to a king bed with brass headboard, there's a day bed in the sitting room. Avocet evokes the exotic with its Oriental reds, cream, and black color palette. A balcony overlooks the garden. Spacious Curlew is fitted with a small kitchenette, a queen sleeper sofa, and a queen bed, while a private outdoor deck is shaded by a large oak tree. Guillemot—the largest room, with a high, vaulted redwood ceiling—has a fireplace and extensive brass accents that perpetuate a nautical motif. This is our prime-pick for honeymooners and other romantic occasions. With wicker furniture and a queen bed, Osprey is brilliant with its blue and white décor and vintage redwood paneling. Pelican, a private cottage surrounded by a garden with a profusion of roses, appropriately features floral motifs, a corner fireplace, sitting area and a king bed.

Gourmet breakfast served in the spacious dining room and under the covered veranda includes crepes, fritattas, sausage, and potatoes. The 213 signature-dish is a stuffed French toast prepared the night before. The owners, innkeepers, and staff are an integral and essential factor in why the Inn is such an attractive place to stay, but equally enticing is the classic architecture, elegant interior finishes, and the garden setting. A bonus is the locale—the Inn is conveniently located within comfortable walking distance to the beach, golfing, and exploring the enchanting village of Pacific Grove. Come for a relaxing stay at The Inn at 213 Seventeen Mile Drive and savor the inviting charms of Pacific Grove.

Marina Dunes

3295 Dunes Drive
Marina, CA 93933
Telephone: 831-883-9478
Reservations: 877-944-3863
www.marinadunes.com

Highlights

♦ Resort set on 19-acre secluded stretch of Monterey Bay Dunes, steps from the beach

♦ Mobil Three-Star and AAA Three-Diamond resort

♦ 60 bungalows with 20 ocean-facing units situated amidst the dunes

♦ Massage and spa services, yoga on the beach, beachside weddings and receptions

♦ On-site restaurant, AJ Spurs, serves award-winning Western cuisine

♦ No cars allowed in dune-front area of resort—you're provided with a cart for the duration of your stay

♦ Two ADA handicapped-accessible units

♦ Rates from $89 to $399 (add $15 per night, per room for Dunes Restoration fee)

Situated ten minutes from bustling Monterey, Marina Dunes Resort—nestled on the coastal dune's undulating flanks—offers a distinctive destination experience. After spending the day traipsing through Fisherman's Wharf, Cannery Row, and among the throngs of strolling tourists in downtown Carmel, the solace of Marina Dunes is welcomed and savored.

MARINA DUNES BEACH

Marina Dunes is the ideal destination if you're in pursuit of relaxation and the rejuvenating powers of the Pacific Ocean. Be sure to request one of the ocean-facing bungalow suites—they are smartly designed to provide maximum insulation and isolation and they're literally set front-row-center with panoramic vistas of the dunes and Monterey Bay.

Settled in our suite, the first thing we did was to slide back the plantation shutters, draw open the slider and relax on the outdoor patio—savoring the sounds of crashing waves and sea birds soaring overhead. We were quickly lulled into the comforting illusion that the nearest neighbor was miles away. After dinner we returned for a reprise session on the deck, champagne in hand, of course. The lights of Cannery Row and the Wharf in Monterey winked like stars nesting on the distant shore, while across Monterey Bay to the north we could see the lights of Santa Cruz.

John King, owner and visionary developer or Marina Dunes, spent years designing and refining this ecologically sensitive resort concept. King did a masterful job of mirroring the timeless California Coastal agrarian-style of architecture by utilizing board-and-batten siding, low-slung gable-form shingle roofs and twin tower-structures that powerfully emulate the ubiquitous farmstead water-tower.

Another distinguishing attribute at Marina Dunes is that there are no cars or car parks in the oceanfront area of the resort. When you arrive, in addition to room keys, you're issued a golf cart for the duration of your stay. A valet initially escorts you to your room, but then you are free to putter about the property in your own cart.

All of the dune-front bungalows are exceptionally spacious with gas-log fireplaces. Oversized bathrooms include double vanities and separate tubs and showers. King size beds, CD players, TVs, wet-bars, terry robes, and rich leather upholstered chairs, as well as marble-top writing desks, are notable in-room elements that harmonize to create an inviting and relaxing home away from home.

On-site amenities include two heated pools, an oversized hot tub, a full array of spa services (either in massage rooms at the main lodge building or en suite by prior arrangement), croquet, volleyball, and—most popular of all—beach walks along the famed shoreline of Monterey Bay. Off-site activities include biking, kayaking, world-class golf, hang gliding, surfing, wine tasting, gallery hopping, and whale watching excursions.

Coupled with easy proximity to Monterey and Carmel, the distinguishing allure of Marina Dunes Resort is the stunning setting in the dunes—and of course the romantic, ocean-facing bungalow suites.

Santa Cruz & Half Moon Bay

Inn at Depot Hill

250 Monterey Avenue
Capitola-by-the-Sea, CA 95010
Telephone: 408-462-3376
www.innatdepothill.com

Highlights

- Originally constructed in 1901 as Pacific Coast Railroad passenger and freight depot

- Mobil Four-Star and AAA Four-Diamond resort

- Theme rooms from route of Orient Express and other exotic destinations

- Lavish baths with Jacuzzis

- Two blocks to village and beach

- Evening wine and cheese, hors d'oeuvres, desert, and late-night cookies

- Rates from $245 to $385 (value season savings of 25 to 35 percent), including full breakfast

Once upon a time, vacationing families from the San Francisco Bay Area commonly traveled to Capitola via passenger trains pulled by wheezing and hissing steam engines. Passenger service was curtailed years ago, though, and Southern Pacific sold the old train depot for $1 in 1958. The station would function as a private residence throughout the next three decades.

Local investors purchased the one-time Central Coast Railroad depot in 1989 and embarked upon an extensive, multi-million dollar renovation that resulted in one of the coast's most elegant little inns. A second story was added but many of the original, classic architectural depot-elements remain.

INN AT DEPOT HILL
PATIO

A personal favorite among the inn's abundant special attributes is the cozy living room with its three-sided Victorian-centerpiece pouffe (circular sofa). A grand piano and a large bookshelf highlight the far end of this charming room. Note that the books' checkout policy is distinct from those you'll encounter at most inns. You see, if you like one of the books, the management encourages you to take the volume home with you, for keeps! No charge! You're welcome.

Depot Hill's dining room is another luxurious treat. One small table is set against an interior wall that's painted as a trompe l'oeil dining-car train window, with exterior vistas beyond. Mounted on the wall directly above the dining-car table is an authentic railway suitcase-rack, complete with two stowed pieces of vintage luggage. The main dining table, set in the midst of the ticket office, is bathed with an energizing soft glow of filtered sunlight at breakfast time. For those who prefer breakfast in bed, have no fear—it's the house specialty. But for those who enjoy a breath of fresh air with their morning meal, al fresco seating awaits you on the Inn's spacious brick-lined garden patio. Breakfast is a gourmet affair prepared by the Inn's award-winning chef, while evening treats include wine, hors d'oeuvres, and homemade desserts.

Many of the Depot Hill rooms and suites are named after European towns, three are dubbed in honor of stops along the route of the fabled Orient Express, but one accommodation reflects a local stop. The Capitola Beach Suite is fittingly outfitted with lively California motifs. The Railroad Baron Suite, however, is a fanciful recreation of a 19th century robber baron's luxurious Pullman train car, complete with rich-red upholstered wall coverings, gold leaf, and ornate wood trim. A favorite for honeymooners and lovebirds, Railroad Baron is outfitted with an indoor jacuzzi spa-tub and velvety-plush furnishings, accented with damask and silk.

A stroll down one of the inn's hallways reveals other doors inscribed with names such as Delft, Sissinghurst, Stratford-on-Avon, Paris, Portofino, and Cote D'Azur. Other equally enchanting rooms include Kyoto, Valencia, Costa del Sol, and the three-level Orient Express Suite.

The inn offers an array of extra touches including in-room massages, themed gift baskets, extra flower arrangements, champagne, limos, horse-drawn carriage rides, as well as arranging for a photographer to be present on the beach during a marriage proposal. Other special surprise treats include delivering breakfast in bed—with an engagement ring attached to a croissant, and arranging for local restaurant staff to sing tableside while the gentleman proposes on his knees.

But, even without the special requests, there's plenty of romance built into the inn. For example, every room comes equipped with a fireplace, fresh roses, featherbeds, private patios with two-person hot tubs, and white marble bathrooms with two-spigot showers. If you're celebrating an anniversary or wedding just let the staff know and heart-shaped cookies with your names written on them will be awaiting your in-room arrival. In the morning, breakfast is delivered with special bride-and-groom napkin rings.

Located on Monterey Bay, an hour and a half drive south of San Francisco in Santa Cruz County, the Inn is a two block walk to the beach and numerous shops, boutiques, art galleries and more than 15 restaurants. Next time you have the wanderlust for a trip on the Orient Express, just book a room at the Inn at Depot Hill. It's nearly as romantic, and a lot easier on the pocketbook.

Babbling Brook Inn

1025 Laurel Street
Santa Cruz, CA 90560
Telephone: 831-427-2456
Reservations: 800-866-1131
www.innsbythesea.com

Highlights

◆ Oldest B&B in Santa Cruz

◆ AAA Three-Diamond location

◆ One acre of romantic enchantment

◆ Evening wine and cheese hour and full gourmet breakfast

◆ Walking distance to downtown, beach, and boardwalk

◆ Handicapped accesible

◆ Rates from $180 to $250 (double occupancy; includes breakfast)

Not only is the Babbling Brook the oldest bed and breakfast in the Santa Cruz area, it is also particularly enchanting. Located just a few blocks from the bustle of downtown Santa Cruz, the Babbling Brook is just a three-minute drive to the beach and Boardwalk. The inn is cuddled in a one-acre oasis of towering redwoods, fruit and pine trees, and luminous flowers.

Each room is named after a painter such as Monet, Renoir, or Van Gogh. My room, the Sisley, showcased through French doors the audible beauty of Laurel Creek and its contingency of bird life. An original stone-faced fireplace accents the living room in the main log cabin, adjacent to the front desk. A glass-roofed atrium is set up with linen-covered tables for breakfast and evening wine and cheese. Food and drinks are served buffet-style from sideboards.

BABBLING BROOK RENOIR

Two of my favorite suites are located within the main cottage. The Jonquil—a bedroom intact from the B&B's prior existence as a residence, is highlighted by a queen-size bed and canopy with white eyelet lace, fireplace and skylights, and private bath with shower. Another main-lodge room, The Honeymoon Suite, has a claw-foot tub surrounded with redwood and a four poster, king-size canopy bed. The Honeymoon Suite also has a private deck that overlooks the Babbling Brook's waterfall.

There are eight guest rooms in the two new buildings designed to complement and reflect the original architecture. The Country-French furnishings and finishes of the rooms were picked and placed with such sensitivity that one soon forgets how recently the building was constructed.

Most rooms feature fireplaces, telephones, TV/VCRs, private decks, private baths, and queen-size beds with down comforters. A gourmet breakfast of fresh-squeezed orange juice, coffee, muffins, croissants, and a main dish of the day is served in a cozy parlor where wine and cheese is also served every evening. Throughout the day, coffee and tasty cookies are served in the parlor.

The Ritz-Carlton, Half Moon Bay

One Miramontes Point Rd.
Half Moon Bay, CA 94019
Telephone: 650-712-7000
Reservations: 800-241-3333
www.ritzcarlton.com/resorts/half_moon_bay

Highlights

♦ Overlooks 50 miles of northern California coastline from ocean bluff setting

♦ AAA Five-Diamond location

♦ Navio restaurant features captivating menu of fresh coastal cuisine

♦ Access to two championship golf courses on the grounds

♦ 16,000-square-foot, full-service spa features 16 private treatment rooms

♦ 1,760-square-foot workout facility includes a 760-square-foot aerobics room and heated yoga room

♦ Handicapped accessible

♦ $225 to $3,000

The Ritz-Carlton, Half Moon Bay sits majestically on a private ocean bluff, overlooking 50 miles of northern California coastline and the serene Santa Cruz Mountains. The AAA Five Diamond golf and spa resort boasts 14 acres of private grounds and offers guests every luxury imaginable.

The Ritz-Carlton's exterior evokes memories of the grand seaside lodges of the nineteenth century, with a façade of natural cedar shingles and redwood trellises. Inside, you'll find hardwood floors, redwood accents, large stone fireplaces, and beamed ceilings. Furnishings are covered in the finest cotton and linen fabrics. English antiques blend with Portuguese ceramics

THE RITZ-CARLTON HALF MOON BAY

and tapestries throughout the hotel's main lodge and guesthouses, and a notable art collection of oil paintings, watercolors, and sepia etchings grace the walls.

The 261 guest rooms include 153 deluxe, 50 club-level, 22 suites, and 36 guest-house rooms. In-room amenities include feather bed with duvet, marble bathroom, fully stocked honor bar with refrigerator, patio (on the first and second floors), full-sized desk, three telephones with voice mail and fax outlets, and high-speed Internet access. Two-thirds of all guest rooms offer a breathtaking view of the Pacific ocean.

Guest services include twice-daily maid service and evening turndown service, twenty-four-hour room service, babysitting service, a golf concierge, and more. Fifth-floor guests enjoy special amenities and services on The Ritz-Carlton Club Level. Guests in these 50 rooms enjoy a personal concierge staff; private lounge with spectacular ocean views; and complimentary breakfast, light lunch, afternoon tea and hors d'oeuvres, desserts available all day, and cocktails served throughout the evening.

The Ritz-Carlton Spa offers 16,000 square feet of space and 16 private treatment rooms, including eight single massage rooms, one couples massage room, three facial rooms, and more. Spa guests can relax in the men's and women's lounges, which offer whirlpool, steam room, and sauna facilities. Guests can also relax in the co-ed Roman mineral bath, complete with nearby fireplace and Tsunami showers. The spa also offers an extensive selection of facials, bath care, and massage therapies for individuals and couples.

The hotel offers a range of dining choices, including a restaurant, conservatory, salon, and bar. The centerpiece of these culinary offerings is their signature 122-seat oceanfront restaurant, Navio. Refined wood finishes and coastal views through floor-to-ceiling windows create the sense that one is dining on a nineteenth-century sea vessel.

The Pacific Ocean serves as the perfect backdrop for the Ritz-Carlton, Half Moon Bay. Take in the charm of the beautiful northern California coast as you stroll on the greens, watch powerful waves crash on the rocks below, or relax after a massage. No matter what you do with your time at this resort location, the surrounding beauty and impeccable ambiance and service is bound to take your breath away.

RITZ-CARLTON
ROMAN MINERAL BATH

Half Moon Bay Lodge

2400 S. Cabrillo Highway
Half Moon Bay, CA 94019
Telephone: 650-726-9000
Reservations: 800-710-0778
www.halfmoonbaylodge.com

Highlights

- Three diamond AAA rating

- Multilingual staff (English/Spanish)

- Health club with hot tub, therapy pool, heated outdoor pool, and fitness center

- Nearby fishing, horseback riding, nature preserves, and hiking

- Romantic packages available

- Handicappped accessible

- Rates from $99 to 239, romantic packages from $229 to $299

Though not as upscale as the neighboring Ritz Carlton, the Half Moon Bay Lodge offers its own unique brand of affordable and gracious hospitality. This charming hacienda-style lodge is designed to give the romancing couple both seclusion and opportunities for fun and adventure. The Lodge itself has 80 luxurious guest rooms all set overlooking the Arnold Palmer-designed Half Moon Bay Golf Links, with its two 18-hole courses. Whale watching, horseback riding, diving, kayaking, surfing, art galleries, and antique shopping are all available in the area around the serene seaside village of Half Moon Bay.

Our stay at the Half Moon Bay Lodge was nothing but spectacular. A helpful attendant ushered us into our room, where everything was perfect. Taking advantage of the lodge's Romantic Package, our large and comfortable suite came with a bottle of champagne, the fireplace ready to

HALF MOON BAY LODGE

light, a sumptuous selection of gourmet chocolate, and a gift basket that included massage oil and aromatherapy scents. Leaving our cares behind, we settled into our cozy abode for an evening of relaxation and romance.

The Health and Fitness facilities at the Half Moon Bay Lodge are excellent. The Fitness Center is located next to the pool and spa and includes an array of exercise equipment, including an electronic stair climber, treadmill, and stationary bike. Fresh fruit and daily newspapers are available in the lobby.

Hiking expeditions abound nearby. Two great hiking spots are Purisima Creek Redwoods Open Space Preserve and the Año Nuevo State Reserve.

Año Nuevo State Reserve is the site of the world's largest mainland breeding colony for the northern elephant seal. People who hope to see the seals during the winter breeding season are urged to get their reservations early. The males battle for mates on the beaches and the females give birth to their pups on the dunes. During the breeding season, December through March, daily access to the reserve is available via guided walks only.

Talk to the knowledgeable concierge at the lodge about all that's available to do in the area. White sand beaches stretch out along the coast around Half Moon Bay, and the small town offers an array of shops, galleries, and restaurants for you to discover. And if you desire big city night life, you can skip over to San Francisco for a night on the town and be back in Half Moon Bay in about a half an hour.

This makes the Half Moon Bay Lodge an ideal romantic getaway, offering pristine coastline, world class golf, and small town charm close to sophisticated metro entertainment.

Half Moon Bay guest room

Cypress Inn

407 Mirada Road
Half Moon Bay, CA 94019
Telephone: 650-726-6002
Reservations: 800-832-3224
www.innsbythesea.com

Highlights

♦ Contemporary oceanside rooms, most with unobstructed views and private decks

♦ In-house masseuse and massage studio, new rooms featuring ocean views from oversize Jacuzzis, and other unusual extras

♦ Gourmet breakfasts, elaborate late afternoon hors d'ouvres, and enticing snacks available 24-hours

♦ Extremely friendly, long-term staff

♦ Four wheelchair-accessible rooms

♦ 18 cozy rooms

♦ Rates from $180 to $365

May the moon and stars bring you a night of sweet dreams." These are the words printed on a small indigo-colored box, placed on your pillow at turndown, when you stay at the Cypress Inn. Inside are two chocolates, one shaped like a star and the other like a crescent moon.

But with a featherbed to snuggle up in, and the sound of the ocean outside your door, you may well wonder whether it's possible *not* to have sweet dreams here. Certainly the small, friendly staff does everything possible to make sure you do. Most of them have been here several years, and are largely responsible for the fact that almost 70 percent of the clientele are returning guests.

Cypress Inn

The Cypress Inn is located less than an hour's drive from San Francisco, directly across the road from five miles of white sand on Miramar Beach. Its three buildings—Main House, Beach House, and the just completed Lighthouse—offer informal yet stylish rooms, many with unobstructed ocean views. All rooms have decks, fireplaces, private bathrooms, featherbeds, TVs, and phones.

The inn's public rooms are in the Main House. Here breakfast is served at a long pine table (although it can also be delivered to your room) and a huge living room beckons with cushy sofas, large skylights, and a tile fireplace. In winter, chestnuts by the fire make rainy or blustery days extra romantic.

The inn's original eight rooms, also in the Main House, share a Mexican motif and are named in Spanish for the earth's natural elements: El Cielo (the sky), El Viento (the wind), and so forth. The Main House guestrooms are not grand in size, but large enough, and utterly charming. Their casual, folkloric style includes wooden animals from Oaxaca, tile floors, natural wood and wicker furniture, and pretty pastel-colored walls and fabrics. Beach House and Lighthouse offer the same amenities as the Main House, but with some differences in style and features.

Beach House, built behind Main House, has four rooms, all on the second floor—accessed via a stairway painted with an enchanting mural of local sea life. Three of the rooms have partial ocean views. The fourth, Venice Beach, is whimsically decorated in a blue and white nautical motif—for its ocean view, a trompe l'oiel ocean scene painted on one wall must suffice.

Across the street, in the Lighthouse, are the inn's six newest and most luxurious rooms. The four front rooms have unobstructed ocean views, and the two rear ones have fine north and south coastal views. Warm teal and honey color carpets merge with tile. Best of all, for the ultimate in romance deep oversize Jacuzzis are placed not in the bathroom, but in the bedroom. They are arranged so that no one can see you, while you enjoy the view, the fireplace … and each other.

Many inns offer complimentary hors d'ouvres, but the Cypress Inn treats guests to a gourmet repast. Ours included pesto pizza with pine nuts and sun-dried tomatoes, "exotic" fruit, a variety of olives, marinated artichoke hearts, several kinds of cheese and crackers, sparkling cider, and wine.

Even if you miss the hors d'ouvres, you won't go hungry. Cookies and fruit are always available in the lobby, as well as coffee, tea, and hot chocolate. A pastry chef comes in a couple times a week to prepare luscious desserts, such as pecan caramel cheesecake. Dessert comes out of the kitchen at 7:30 and stays out all night.

Breakfast is equally hearty and delicious. Peaches-and-cream French toast is the Sunday special. Other days bring tasty treats such as peach parfait layered with granola, crustless quiche with sour cream sauce, fresh baked breads, and fresh-squeezed orange juice.

Most people come to this quiet spot just to relax, but the area right outside the inn's door is worth exploring. A five-minute stroll along the beach will take you past an odd but architecturally interesting mix of buildings including the Bach Dynamite and Dancing Society, a beachfront "party house" featuring live jazz and classical music concerts by world-renowned artists. Whether it's beachcombing, or just savoring the quietude and majestic vistas from your room, Cypress Inn is a prime destination for romance along the California Coast.

San Francisco Bay Region

The Hayes Mansion
Conference Center

200 Edenvale Avenue
San Jose, CA 95136
Telephone: 408-226-3200
Reservations: 800-420-3200
www.hayesmansion.com

Highlights

♦ Quick escape from city life (15 minutes from downtown San Jose)

♦ Beautifully restored century-old mansion with timeless architecture

♦ Lush grounds adjacent to a 20-acre park

♦ Resort-like facilities including elegant restaurant

♦ Idyllic setting for weddings and receptions

♦ Three wheelchair-accessible rooms

♦ 140 rooms. Rates from $135 to $700

The Hayes Mansion leads a double life. During the week, it's a conference center with all the business amenities you'd expect in a first-class Silicon Valley hotel. On the weekends, it's a peaceful Mediterranean-style retreat offering a quick and easy escape from the everyday world, a place where you can enjoy resort-like facilities that include a restaurant, swimming pool, tennis and volleyball courts, jogging paths, and nearby golf courses. The room rates are about the same as a good massage, so even locals can splurge on a stay here without feeling guilty.

Set back on wide, manicured lawns behind a flower-lined circular driveway and soaring palms, the mansion is an historic landmark. Built by the socially prominent Hayes family in 1905, it soon became the center of Santa Clara county society. Mary Hayes, the family matriarch, was a faith-healer who at

THE HAYES MANSION

one point had 3,000 patients, and her two sons were politically active. In its heyday, the mansion attracted visiting presidents William McKinley, Theodore Roosevelt, and Herbert Hoover, as well as other luminaries of the time.

In 1975, the mansion was listed on the National Register of Historic Places. In1981, after years of disrepair, it was declared a city landmark and purchased for restoration to its original splendor.

In 1994, the mansion was completely renovated and greatly expanded. Care was taken to preserve, whenever possible, the original features, such as wood floors and lighting fixtures. Historic photos of the mansion's fascinating past are scattered throughout the halls and public rooms.

The guest rooms reflect the property's business orientation with a sedate, slightly masculine look. Though not particularly imaginative, they are extremely comfortable, spacious, and yes, even luxurious. Our suite had a huge terrace with umbrella table and chairs, as well as a separate sitting room with a second TV and wet bar. Everything seemed ergonomically correct, with all the switches in the right places, good lighting, and a nice, deep tub, complete with bubble bath, to relax in before bed.

An exception to the no-frills décor is the lovely Cypress Suite, which features a clawfoot tub and a view of the hills. This would be the room to reserve for an especially romantic evening. In fact, many weddings are held on the hotel's lush grounds, with the Cypress Suite the favorite choice for the "bridal suite."

The suites on the top floor of the historic wing make cozy hideaways. All except one have pedestal tubs and separate showers, separate sitting areas, video players and stereos, and wet bars.

A highlight of our stay was a leisurely lunch in the hotel's elegant Orlo's Restaurant. With original built-in furniture and tapestry wall covering identical to the original, this old-fashioned room evokes the graciousness of a bygone era. The menu changes daily, and many dishes feature freshly picked herbs from the mansion's gardens. The moderately-priced specialties include grilled pork medallions with white peach gastrique, pine nut and garlic crusted halibut, and vegetable linguine with spicy asparagus and wild mushrooms.

During the day, you can laze around the enormous pool, just wander the grounds, or pursue the other recreational options at the hotel or nearby. If you feel the need for some urban stimulation, downtown San Jose is a 15-minute drive away, and the hotel concierge will helpfully map out an itinerary for you. Once there, though, chances are you'll wish you'd never left this quiet getaway with the very affordable price.

The Hayes Mansion
Romantic Bath

Mandarin Oriental San Francisco

222 Sansome Street
San Francisco, CA 94104-2792
Telephone: 415-276-9888
www.mandarinoriental.com/hotel

Highlights

◆ San Francisco's only Mobil Five-Star hotel (2000, 2001, 2002)

◆ Located in the heart of the city. A pleasant walk to shopping, theaters, and galleries and a fun cable car ride to Nob Hill and Fisherman's Wharf

◆ Spectacular views of the city and/or bay from every guestroom

◆ Impeccable and gracious service in the tradition of the hotel's flagship property in Hong Kong

◆ Award-winning Silks Restaurant serving contemporary American cuisine with a Pacific Rim influence

◆ Two luxurious suites that boast 1,000-square-foot private terraces for breathtaking views of the city, bay, and famous landmarks

◆ Handicapped accessible

◆ Rates from $470 to $725 (single); suites from $1,400 to $3,000

Is it possible? A sophisticated, international corporate-business hotel thriving as a world-class love nest in the heart of San Francisco's frenetic Financial District?

The answer is a resounding "yes." I know this because my wife, Beth, and I honeymooned at the Mandarin, indulgently sequestered in a magnificent suite on the 39th floor.

The Mandarin occupies the top 11 floors of the third tallest building in the city, and this is a key to its allure. You are so high up that when you

MANDARIN ORIENTAL

look down on Nob Hill, you're eye level with the top of the Transamerica Pyramid. The view personifies the word panoramic—Berkeley, the Golden Gate, Alcatraz, Angel Island, Sausalito, Mt. Tammopolis, the Richmond-San Rafael Bridge, Treasure Island, Chinatown, Fisherman's Wharf, Coit Tower, and every other conceivable vista associated with the City-by-the-Bay is spread before you (binoculars are a standard amenity in every room).

Beth still fondly recalls a relaxing session in the palatial bathroom's deep soaking tub. Illuminated with floor-to-ceiling picture windows, it was a snap to draw her bath water but an entirely different matter to draw her back out. All bathrooms feature European-style bathtubs with hand held shower, separate oversized shower, a television/speaker system installed under the vanity, plush oversized towels from Bangkok, bathrobes, and slippers.

The furnishings and bedding are fit for royalty. But, a gold-plated palace is nothing without commensurate service, and this is where the Mandarin shines the brightest. I would come back to stay again, even if the rooms were tattered and threadbare, as long as the same staffers were still on hand to make us feel so very special and welcome. Tom Cheung, a bellman who's worked at the Mandarin Oriental since opening day, was given a special Mobil Five-Star award called "Best of the Best" for excellent service in 2001.

From the moment we arrived to the minute we departed, the incredibly gracious and accommodating service continued non-stop. The same smiling valet who'd greeted us upon arrival tucked us in our car as we departed two days later.

The Mandarin's delectable culinary offerings would be reason enough to make a date at this location. After having shared a superb dinner and two incredible desserts, we even requested a doggie bag for the bread. The waiter didn't flinch or smirk at our request; he grinned and confessed that he, too, takes home morsels of Mandarin bread at the end of the evening.

Apparently, there are many others who share our love of the Mandarin Oriental. *Mobil Travel Guide* bestowed the prestigious Five-Star Award to the Mandarin. *Condé Nast Traveler's* Annual Readers' Poll ranks the Mandarin as one of the Best Places to Stay in the World, and the Number One Hotel in San Francisco for rooms and service.

The Mandarin also offers a twist on English high tea. Afternoon Asian tea service in the Mandarin Lounge is served from three to five P.M. daily. Choose from an array of teas from Mighty Leaf Tea Company. Tea service cuisine is presented in a black bento box with four compartments featuring Mandarin Canapés, Thai Curried Beef Phyllo Triangles, Unagi and Avocado Amaki, and a selection of fine confections. Chopsticks and embroidered silk napkins enhance the Asian afternoon tea experience.

The hotel's concierge service is very accommodating. They can arrange for in-room massages, a day at the spa, a gourmet picnic in Napa, great shopping expeditions, a romantic dinner at Silks, a walk along the Embarcadero under the lights of the Bay Bridge, and more.

MANDARIN ORIENTAL BAYVIEW KING

The Huntington Hotel
and Nob Hill Spa

1075 California Street
San Francisco, CA 94108
Telephone: 415-474-5400
Reservations: 800-227-4683
www.huntingtonhotel.com

Highlights

♦ Small Luxury Hotels of the World and Preferred Hotels & Resorts member

♦ 100 rooms and 35 suites featuring elegant design and decor

♦ Complimentary chauffeur service within the city

♦ In room fax, DSL Internet, wet bar or kitchen, signature soaps and lotions

♦ Complimentary tea or sherry served in your room upon arrival

♦ Nob Hill Spa facility with ten treatment rooms (three with fireplaces) and indoor pool

♦ Breathtaking vistas and an extensive wellness program (inquire about the Romance and Relaxation package)

♦ Handicapped accessible

♦ Rates from $300 to $445 (double occupancy); suites from $475 to $1,125

THE HUNTINGTON HOTEL POOL

The Huntington is considered one of the crown jewels of Nob Hill, presiding over San Francisco's most prestigious summit with quiet confidence. Originally developed in the days of the notorious robber barons, Nob Hill has remained the province of the privileged—a testimony to wealth and power. Today, it is still San Francisco's most coveted address.

From the moment one is greeted by the affable doorman and escorted to the reception desk, it is quite clear that service is a way of life at the Huntington Hotel. Each member of the staff is gracious and accommodating without a trace of pretension. The Huntington offers indulgence without imposition—truly impeccable service.

The Huntington's discreet entrance opens to a spacious lobby. The decor has a distinctly residential feel, a characteristic that is echoed in the 135 guest rooms. Dark woods are polished to a lustrous sheen and complement the fine fabrics—damasks, watered silks, and brocades in rich jewel tones.

The guest rooms are decorated in three distinctive styles and reflect the refined spirit of the property. Suites are individually appointed. Each room features an electronic safe, large antique desk, radio, cable TV, voice mail, and high-speed Internet access. Baths are spacious marble sanctuaries, and terry cloth bathrobes are available upon request.

Dining is an exquisite experience at the Huntington. The hotel's Big Four restaurant, adjacent to the lobby, is a recommended choice for local diners as well as hotel guests. Named for the four railroad tycoons who ruled the heady heights of Nob Hill (Hopkins, Crocker, Stanford, and Huntington), the restaurant is a living tribute to that halcyon era. It is a study in masculine elegance; dark woods and etched mirrors grace the walls, accented by early Western railroad memorabilia, and muted lighting glows subtly from curved sconces along the walls. The dark green leather banquettes and brass-studded armchairs recall a gentleman's smoking room; and at night, it becomes just that. The prolific pianist plays tasteful tunes, which delight the after-opera crowd, and the air is fragrant with the smoke of fine cigars.

A recent addition to the Huntington's litany of superlatives, the Nob Hill Spa offers an assortment of custom-tailored treatments, including Asian, Ashi, and Longevity. Award-winning spa cuisine is served daily on an outdoor terrace. Inquire about the Wellness Program's Guided Meditation, Chi Kung, and Pilates mat classes. Also, be sure to find out about the special overnight Romance and Relaxation package.

Mark Hopkins Intercontinental

Number One Nob Hill
(999 California Street)
San Francisco, CA 94108
Telephone: 415 392 3434
www.san-francisco.intercontinental.com

Highlights

◆ Top of the Mark, the world-renowned 19th-floor sky lounge with spectacular views of the San Francisco Bay area.

◆ AAA Four-Diamond location

◆ Gold Key Award

◆ 380 guest rooms, including 39 suites, five of which are luxury suites; seven suites have glass-enclosed terraces, which are unique to San Francisco

◆ Highly personalized service, attention to detail, well-trained and multilingual staff

◆ The Nob Hill Restaurant features masterful interpretations of contemporary classic cuisine

◆ Handicapped accessible

◆ Rates from $335 to $7,750

In what is often hailed as the most romantic city in North America, the premier landmark of San Francisco is Nob Hill. The area's reputation of privilege dates back to Gold Rush times, when railroad barons and Gold Rush kings built their mansions in this exclusive spot. Today, luxury hotels now stand in the place of those original palaces, and at the exclusive address of Number One Nob Hill you encounter one of the city's most treasured jewels: The Mark Hopkins Intercontinental Hotel.

Mark Hopkins Intercontinental

The Mark Hopkins has been a landmark since its opening in 1926 on the site of the former 40-room mansion of Mark Hopkins, founder of the Southern Pacific Railroad. The original Hopkins home was destroyed in the 1906 earthquake and fire. The property changed hands a few times before hotel investor George Smith bought it and built a luxury hotel on this special piece of land.

The Mark Hopkins has been at the center of San Francisco's rich history. Events such as the meetings for the historic founding of the United Nations in 1945 took place at the Mark Hopkins. Royalty, statesmen, political personalities, and celebrities have found refuge at the Mark Hopkins.

For those seeking romance, the Mark Hopkins fulfills every desire. From the moment you arrive, you are immersed in its elegance.

Upon entering the Lobby, guests are surrounded by a wonderfully inviting ambience. Copper-toned upholstered walls play off the original 1926 marble flooring throughout the room. Sumptuous fabrics—chenille, tapestries, cut velvets—cover custom-made furniture in rich, contemporary hues of aubergine, warm blues, and honey-wheat browns. Comfortable sofas and overstuffed chairs are arranged in intimate settings on hand-woven carpets.

Guest rooms highlight the mix of traditional and modern. The sumptuous One-Bedroom Suites exhibit the hotel's elegance and attention to detail. All suites offer whirlpool baths to soothe body and soul.

Unique to San Francisco hotels, the Mark Hopkins features seven Terrace Suites with glass-enclosed patios that further highlight the panoramic views of the city and the Bay area. Five luxury suites, located on the top three floors of the hotel, offer distinctively different styles from each other, with designs inspired by the American, European, and Asian influences on San Francisco. Each offers something unique—some have solariums, some have a formal dining room, some have fireplaces—in addition to the luxury of materials and gracious setting. All the luxury suites have jacuzzi tubs. The Terrace Suites make for the ultimate in romanantic refuge.

From the Mark Hopkins, all of San Francisco lays at your feet, ready for exploration, knowing that at the end of your day you will be welcomed home by the hotel's hospitable ambience and exceptional staff. Then find your way to the Top of the Mark, the quintessential San Francisco landmark for lovers, where you can dine, dance, and romance amidst the stars and the lights of the City by the Bay.

Nightscape on top of Mark Hopkins

Campton Place Hotel

340 Stockton St.
San Francisco, CA 94108
Telephone: 415-781-5555
Reservations: 800-235-4300
www.camptonplace.com

Highlights

- Excellent downtown San Francisco location adjacent to famed Union Square shopping district

- Rare blend of sophistication and intimacy, recently enhanced by $15 million renovation.

- Restaurant voted number one for "best hotel food in the U.S." by *Condé Nast Traveler*, Hotel Ranked number ten of the top 30 North American hotels and AAA Five-Diamond award for both hotel and restaurant

- Discreet elegance with attentive, professional staff concierge services, 24-hour room-service, valet assistance with unpacking

- High speed T-1 Internet connection, Bose Wave radio, CD player

- Luxury suites available for receptions

- Member of Leading Small Hotels of the World

- Four wheelchair-accessible rooms

- Rates from $340 to $475; suites from $575 to $2,050

Location, location, location. As realtors tell us, location is all. And in San Francisco, what better location for your touring base than Union Square? This is where you'll find some of the city's best theater venues, trendy boutiques, art galleries, and restaurants. Fisherman's Wharf, Chinatown, North Beach and other world-famous neighborhoods are just minutes away.

THE CAMPTON PLACE HOTEL GUEST ROOM

This is also where you'll find one of the city's premiere hotels, Campton Place. Of course, there are other places to stay on or near Union Square, but few offer the same winning blend of sophistication and intimacy. And no other hotel can compete with Campton Place Restaurant, named number one for "best hotel food in the United States" by *Condé Nast Traveler* magazine (January 2000). But more on that later.

First, the service is highly professional, courteous and knowledgeable. Limousine service, overnight shoeshine, and a state-of-the-art fitness center are all complimentary. There's even a concierge available 24 hours to help you make the most of your time in "America's favorite city."

In late 2000 the hotel completed a $15 million renovation of all 110 guest rooms and suites. Although the sizes and locations of accommodations vary, they share a similar décor and even the smaller rooms are so well designed that they seem spacious. The look is uncluttered, understated elegance, with an emphasis on modern design and comfort. Distinctive features include custom-made pear wood armoires stenciled with a silver leaf motif, furniture reproductions of Chippendale and Louis XVI periods, silk fabrics, and leather top writing desks. Some have cozy window seats or fireplaces. All accommodations feature featherbeds and thermo-pane glass to help you drift off to sleep in silent luxury.

The bathrooms follow the European open style and are sleekly handsome with limestone floors and countertops. Amenities include lightweight, terry cloth robes and slippers and Crabtree & Evelyn toiletries.

Like the hotel, Campton Place Restaurant is upscale yet personal. The dining room is decorated in soothing peach and gold, softly lit, with white linen tables and plush velvet banquettes. Although it was full by 7P.M., we could still hear each other without shouting. The staff was gracious and unobtrusive. On request, our waiter described to us the ingredients and cooking methods of the various dishes.

The restaurant serves "contemporary Mediterranean food". Dishes such as Breast of Sonoma Squab, boned and plumped with artichokes, olives, sun-dried tomatoes and basil then covered with a basket weave of strips of zucchini and Sauteed Calamari stuffed with ratatouille and garnished with fried parsley are unlike any others you'll find in the City. We sample these delectable offerings and several more on the tasting menu for $145 ($85 without wine).

The food is beautifully presented and worthy of its rave reviews. You could easily spend two or three hours here, for this is a meal to be savored. For a nightcap, you can stop off at the adjacent Campton Place Bar.

When we returned to the restaurant for breakfast, we mentioned to our waitress how impressed we'd been with dinner. "Good," she said, "because we make a dining experience out of breakfast."

She was right—breakfast was served with the same finesse as dinner. She added that some locals drop by regularly, just for the French toast and hot chocolate. I can vouch for the hot chocolate—the best I've ever tasted, almost like melted chocolate—not too sweet, but just right, like everything about Campton Place.

The Argent Hotel

50 Third Street
San Francisco, California 94103
Telephone: 415-974-6400
Reservations: 877-222-6699
www.argenthotel.com

Highlights

♦ Located in the heart of San Francisco's trendy new South of Market area (SOMA)

♦ AAA Four-Diamond location

♦ Jester's Restaurant boasting one of only two French master chefs in San Francisco

♦ 667 guest rooms and 26 suites all with floor-to-ceiling views of the city

♦ Handicapped accessible

♦ Rates from $179 to $349

Located in San Francisco's trendy new downtown, the buzzing South of Market area, The Argent Hotel prides itself on being in the "right place." Since it is just steps from the San Francisco Museum of Modern Art, Sony's Metreon Entertainment Complex, Union Square, Yerba Buena Gardens, the Giants-Pacific Bell Park, and the Theatre District, it's a hard assertion to dispute. But the Argent doesn't just boast location; it also offers first-class accommodations. Each of the Argent's 667 spacious guest rooms and 26 suites offer breathtaking floor-to-ceiling panoramic views of the city and artistic contemporary furnishings customized with modern elegance in mind. Each room is decorated with original artwork and custom furnishings and features an art deco design motif, giving Argent guests a taste of the essence of urban sophistication.

THE ARGENT GUEST ROOM

The Argent's impeccable sense of style is not limited to its guest rooms; you'll find it pervades every corner of the hotel. A marble-floored foyer leads to the Argent's elegant lobby; there, and throughout the establishment, you'll find rich, intricate woodwork; gold-leaf domes; and a world-class, multi-million dollar art collection gracing the hotel's walls.

For some well deserved self indulgance, the hotel offers a full-service health club and an on-site masseuse service. Surrounded by walls of windows, The Argent Health Club offers Paramount's state-of-the-art cardiovascular and weight machines, as well as stereos, televisions, fully-equipped locker rooms, showers, and saunas. For a massage, guests can choose to relax under the hands of on-site professionals in the privacy of their own room or in a special room located near the health club.

Business people will undoubtedly feel they've come to the right place at the Argent—the top four floors of the hotel are dedicated to business accommodations, with over 20,000 square feet of business and meeting space and sixteen spacious and elegant boardrooms, meeting rooms, and ballrooms. The Argent is the perfect location for a business meeting or retreat of any size. Whether it's 12 or 1,200, the Argent is ready to accommodate you in style and elegance. Executive Level perks include rooms equipped with full-sized lighted desks, three telephones with data port and voice mail, and high-speed in-room Internet service. On the second floor, a full-service business and Internet center offers guests the convenience of an "office on the road," with PC computer rental, photocopying, faxing, and mailing and packaging service.

Jester's Restaurant and Lounge serves up moderately priced American cuisine with a French flair. The French master chef's lunch entrées range from $10.50 to $18.00, dinner entrées from $13.00 to $23.00. Jester's is a showcase of true international luxury and boasts the hippest lounge in the South of Market area. It features live nightly jazz, a sophisticated and swanky atmosphere, and an impressive specialty martini menu, including "Peaches 'n Cream-tini" and "Spicytini" selections.

It's hard to separate business from pleasure at the Argent. Whether you're there for one, the other, or both, you will have no problem answering their favorite question, "Have you ever been at the right place at the right time?" with no hesitation.

East Brother Light Station, Inc.

117 Park Place
Richmond, California 94801
Reservations: 510-233-2385
www.ebls.com

Highlights

♦   Stunningly beautiful 1870s lighthouse and keepers quarters on a little rock islet in San Francisco Bay

♦   Overnight stays, available Thursday through Sunday nights

♦   Ten-minute private launch shuttle from shore

♦   Spectacular vistas of San Francisco skyline Mount Tamalpais above Marin

♦   Library, parlor, dining room, five bedrooms

♦   Operated, restored, and maintained by the non-profit Richmond-based East Brother Light Station Organization

♦   No handicapped accessibility

♦   Rates from $290 to $410 includes boat shuttle, overnight accommodations for two, gourmet dinner, wine and cheese, and full breakfast

We first discovered East Brother Light Station by pure happenstance while motoring by boat from San Francisco to Sacramento. As our boat skimmed through San Pablo Strait in the northern reaches of San Francisco Bay we passed an incredibly beguiling Victorian era lighthouse crowning a tiny rock islet a quarter mile offshore.

A man, whom she presumed to be the keeper, trundled rapidly from the main house and stepped inside a small shed. Just in the knick of time, he

East Brother Light Station from the water

greeted the boat's passing with a reverberating blast-from-the-past "beeee-oooooh" toot of the old Diaphone compressed-air driven foghorn. The vessel's skipper honked out a reply and casually mentioned that the lighthouse now functions as a bed and breakfast.

Smitten by the mystique of the stunningly romantic little lighthouse hunkered in the middle of San Francisco Bay, we vowed to someday come back and stay at this unique maritime B&B.

We were delighted to discover, firsthand, that the fully operational lighthouse has stood sentry over the chilly bay waters for well over one hundred years. The Victorian-era building turned B&B has non-profit-organization status the monies from which—along with a cadre of nearby-area volunteers—are utilized to preserve the island.

There are four comfortable rooms (Marin, San Francisco, Two Sisters and West Brother) in the former lighthouse keeper's quarters—each with a queen-size bed and excellent bay views. Another smaller room, dubbed Walter's Quarters (named for a former keeper), is located in the detached fog signal building.

Accommodations include shore-side parking, a ten-minute boat shuttle to the island and back, hors d'oeuvres with champagne, an excellent four-course dinner with complimentary wine, a full gourmet breakfast and a tour of the light station. In addition to romantic getaways, the Light Station may also be reserved for weddings, receptions and small corporate retreats.

Overnight guests are picked up at 4 P.M. sharp at the San Pablo Yacht Harbor. Morning checkout and launch back to the mainland is at 11:00 A.M.

If you're looking for utter solitude with a twist, this is the place for you. What an experience in the middle of the bay!

EAST BROTHER LIGHT STATION EXTERIOR

The Inn Above Tide

30 El Portal
Sausalito, CA 94965
Telephone: 415 332 9535
Reservations: 800 893 8433
www.innabovetide.com

Highlights

♦ Unique location on San Francisco Bay with breathtaking views of the city skyline

♦ Steps away from the San Francisco ferry

♦ Stylish contemporary rooms with deluxe amenities, often including private decks and fireplaces

♦ Wine and cheese hour

♦ Expanded continental breakfast

♦ Three wheelchair-accessible rooms

♦ Rates from $265 to $465; suites from $495 to $865

For a view of San Francisco Bay "up close and personal," there's only one place to stay: The Inn Above Tide. As the brochure says, "There are hundreds of hotels located around San Francisco Bay. There is, however, only one on it." Sleek and sophisticated, the new, three-story Inn Above Tide is built over the water next to the ferry landing, with an unobstructed bay view from every room. Floor-to-ceiling windows take full advantage of the inn's unique location.

You're dazzled by water everywhere as soon as the room door opens. From the private glass-walled deck, stretch out on a chaise lounge and—armed with binoculars courtesy of the inn—be ready for some serious viewing. Sailboats, kayaks, yachts, and motorboats ply the waters; the Red and White fleet comes so close you can almost jump on board. In the distance sits San

The Inn Above Tide tub view

Francisco, Alcatraz, and the Tiburon hills. The sunsets are magical, and when stars begin to twinkle the scene dons a majesty all of its own.

The subdued decor at Inn Above Tide is designed to enhance the views; some even sport porthole windows. Renovated in 2004, guest rooms are patterned in rich, earthy tones. A typical room features oversized chairs and ottomans, a luxuriously covered king-size bed with playfully shaped pillows and a stone fireplace. The large bathrooms have deep oval tubs stocked with the inn's lavender bath salts. All rooms feature wireless Internet connections and generous amenities, while the spacious, newly designed suite is also arrayed with a Jacuzzi and two plasma TVs.

Breakfast, which can be delivered roomside if preferred, consists of a deliciously plentiful assortment of freshly baked goods, fresh fruit and juices, yogurt, granola, and beverages.

Sausalito and the surrounding area offer everything you can imagine in the way of outdoor activities. A trek across the Golden Gate Bridge is almost a "must do," but there are also beautiful beach and hiking options a short drive away at Mt. Tamalpais, Muir Woods, Stinson Beach, and Point Reyes.

Equally enjoyable cultural activities are also easily found nearby. Sausalito village is home to many local artisans and its galleries house a wonderful collection of both local and internationally created art.

There are many fine establishments within walking distance but if city-lights dining is a must, you might consider hopping on the ferry for an especially romantic touch.

All things considered, the Inn Above Tide is gifted not only with a spectacular location, but also an elegant, comfortable, and inviting ambience as well. Owner Bill McDevitt seems to agree. He built the property in 1961 as luxury apartments, remodeled it for $3 million, and opened it to guests in late 1995. He wouldn't live anyplace else. "Even the storms are fun," he says. "The water hits our wave baffle and splashes up three stories. It's exciting as hell." And that says it all.

Inn Above Tide room

177

Casa Madrona Hotel

801 Bridgeway
Sausalito, CA 94965
Telephone: 415-332-0502
Reservations: 800-567-9524
www.CasaMadrona.com

Highlights

♦ Magnificent views of San Francisco Bay or the Inn's lush gardens

♦ Award-winning Italian-Tuscan restaurant, Poggio

♦ The Main House is on the National Historic Registry; newer accommodations include 63 Hillside Casita rooms, suites, and cottages

♦ Fanciful theme rooms, with private decks, fireplaces, and oversize tubs

♦ Full service spa, Avanyu

♦ One wheelchair-accessible room

♦ Rates from $255 to 490 year-round (vacation and spa packages available)

Perched on a steep hill in the center of town, the venerable Casa Madrona is a Sausalito landmark, a bit quirky and absolutely delightful. Following the brick walkways way up, down, and around, led to the discovery of a small balcony here, a cozy sitting room there, and unexpected nooks and crannies that added to the distinct character of the place. And around every corner were the spectacular views that bring visitors to Sausalito in the first place.

Built in 1885, the Casa Madrona was a decaying hippie pad when current owner John Mays bought the property in the mid-70s. Mays reinforced the original structure and added 16 rooms. Today guests can stay in the Victorian House, Surrounding Cottages, or Hillside Casitas.

A night's stay in the antique-filled Victorian House's Wicker Room offers country-fresh surroundings in green and white, with an old-fashioned four-

CASA MADRONA HOTEL BATH

poster bed and white wicker furniture. White wood shutters frame the inn's lovely gardens and a bit of the bay as well.

Other rooms are more fanciful. The Katmandu, a Hillside Casita, is filled with large cushions for lounging, tiny alcoves, mirrors, and carpeted steps. With its fireplace, deck, and tub for two, it's ideal for honeymoons and other special occasions.

The Salon Nouveau, another Hillside Casita, is a tribute to art nouveau in lush tones of purple and mauve. Period furnishings include a canopied bed with corded tiebacks and tassels. This romantic room also has a fireplace and a private deck overlooking the bay.

Whimsical or just exceptionally pretty, the rooms at Casa Madrona are always perfectly appointed. Many offer private decks, fireplaces or wood-burning stoves, and oversize tubs. With a room to suit your every mood, this is the kind of place you'll want to return to again and again. No wonder so many people do.

North Coast Region

Meadowood Napa Valley

900 Meadowood Lane
St. Helena, CA 94574
Telephone: 707-963-3646
Reservations: 800-458-8080
www.meadowood.com

Highlights

♦ Unfettered tranquility amidst a 250-acre country estate

♦ Exceptional cuisine and outstanding wine education programs

♦ Nine-hole executive golf course, two world-class croquet courts

♦ Huge pool, Jacuzzi, seven tennis courts, biking, and hiking tours

♦ Perfect home base for Napa/Sonoma winery touring and tasting

♦ Extensive Health Spa facility—a trendsetter in the field

♦ Classical concerts, lectures, seminars, and artist-in-residence programs

♦ Top-notch fitness and exercise program includes personal trainers

♦ 85 spacious suites and cottages, all with enchanting views

♦ Idyllic and ethereal wedding and honeymoon setting

♦ Member: Relais & Chateuax

♦ Handicapped accessible rooms and facilities

♦ Rates from $525 to $3,800

So close and yet so far away—that's what comes to mind whenever I recall my visit to heavenly Meadowood. I first heard of the Napa Valley resort years ago when a concierge at the San Francisco Park Hyatt advised, "You really must go to Meadowood! It is one of California's truly exceptional resort hideaways."

MEADOWOOD GUEST ROOM

Meadowood's litany of upscale amenities includes: a sophisticated high-tech health facility, a nine-hole executive golf course, an award winning restaurant and a multi-court tennis complex. There are hiking trails and a regulation croquet field with a staff croquet professional. However, Meadowood's most essential ingredient has nothing to do with human handiwork. The real magic of this special hideaway is surely the tranquility and serenity of its sylvan setting. *Andrew Harper, Travel & Leisure, Conde Naste Traveler* and other top travel publications regularly rank Meadowood as one of the world's premier resort destinations.

Meadowood is a consummate example of a refined romantic hideaway. The hillside abodes and the main lodge, with dormers and broad verandas, recall the engaging elements of a grand, late nineteenth-century country resort. The cottages are especially seductive, with elegant French doors that open onto private decks, wood-burning fireplaces, rich soft goods, and graceful appointments. In-room amenities include stocked refrigerators, coffee and tea, TVs, fireplaces in most rooms, room service, laundry service, concierge, fresh fruit basket, daily newspaper, hair dryers, and more.

After settling into our suite overlooking the croquet court and golf course, we decided it was time for a Chardonnay massage. The masseuse explained that the "Chardonnay" is actually a non-alcoholic extract combined with essential fatty acids and other natural ingredients that work to rejuvenate the skin and promote skin cell regeneration. In addition to standard, deep tissue, Swedish and the exotic Chardonnay massages, the Spa offers mud treatments, restorative and special "gentlemen's facials," reflexology, weight-loss programs, yoga and stretching classes, personal trainers, body composition analysis, nutritional consultation, aromatherapy and Ayurvedic treatments.

The resort's award-winning eatery is simply called The Restaurant at Meadowood—and it makes perfect sense, as there is absolutely nothing glitzy, stuffy, or pretentious about the cuisine, the staff, or the atmosphere. The masterful culinary creations are presented in a strikingly honest and unpretentious manner. For example the four-course tasting menu offers a plethora of treats such as roast Langoustines (flown in from France) with seared Hudson Valley foie gras and white truffle oil; seared diver scallops with creamy salsify, white truffle and bacon butter; roast loin of venison with savory cabbage, raspberry, and juniper.

If you stay at Meadowood, you can rest assured that the experience will earn a coveted place among your most cherished travel memories.

Manka's Inverness Lodge

30 Callender Way
Inverness, CA 94937
Telephone: 415-669-1034
www.mankas.com

Highlights

- ♦ Popular restaurant featuring locally grown and raised fare

- ♦ Unique and diverse wine list boasting over 150 selections

- ♦ Eight rooms, two cabins, and a suite on the main compound, plus three other accommodations on the waterfront: an 1850s cabin at the water's edge, a dramatic 1911 boathouse built over the water, and the intimate boatman's quarters above the boathouse

- ♦ Surrounded by an 80,000-acre national park

- ♦ Two handicapped accessible rooms

- ♦ Rates from $215 to $565

Not quite one hour north of San Francisco, nestled within 80,000 acres of Point Reyes Peninsula's deep forests and scenic secluded beaches, is Manka's Inverness Lodge, a 1917 hunting and fishing lodge built in the elegantly rustic tradition of the California Arts and Crafts Movement.

Sally Dobbins, the soft-spoken and infinitely gracious host, wastes no time making guests feel right at home from the moment they first step into the main lodge. She greets them with a cup of hot tea and an offer to take a seat by the crackling fire in a cozy room filled with old hickory rockers; vintage fishing gear; and Louie, the lodge Labrador who dozes sleepily on the plaid Craftsman couch.

Manka's Inverness Lodge bath

With Tomales Bay at its feet and the Pacific Ocean at its back, the main property is a small compound of eight rooms, a suite, two cabins, and a widely acclaimed restaurant. Down the road and on the bay you'll find an extension of Manka's offerings, including an 1850s cabin on a couple of acres at the water's edge, a dramatic 1911 boathouse built over the water, and the intimate boatman's quarters above the boathouse.

A centerpiece of Manka's is the restaurant in the main lodge. The chef makes sure the daily menu offers fresh, locally grown fare from some of Manka's closest neighbors, who offer fresh fruits and greens, olives, organic dairy and eggs, and much more. A tender piece of lamb atop creamy herbed polenta is but a sampling of the many offered dishes. Dessert includes homemade caramel vanilla ice cream made with local coastal cream, complete with homemade oatmeal cookie still warm from the oven for dipping.

Manka's also serves up an impressive breakfast, though only to houseguests. You can dine fireside in the parlor (where they grill their own house-made sausages), in your room or cabin, or on your personal deck. When guests wake up, a Provencal offering is brought right to the door consisting of Brie and assorted fresh fruit; homemade pomegranate scone with locally-made whipped butter; and a pot of rich, piping hot coffee. Manka's restaurant has been touted as one of the best restaurants in Northern California by *The Los Angeles Times,* and one can see why. The service and fare at every meal are far beyond exceptional.

Each room, cabin, suite, and other such accommodation that Manka's has dreamed up has its own unique charm, complete with individual color scheme—from Beacon blankets and Pendleton plaids to simple, draped white linen cascading from window to floor. Manka's Cabin would probably be considered the premier haven the Lodge offers. It's like staying in your uncle's woodland hunting cabin, complete with plush, bearskin rug and large stone fireplace. The Cabin offers deep reading chairs and a plaid overstuffed couch to relax in by the fire. The most notable touches were the comfy breakfast nook with bird-watching window and binoculars and the Japanese-style soaking tub on the private deck off the living room. Manka's Cabin also offers a separate bedroom with wide-opening double wooden doors and a shower open to the sky.

With so much to offer, Manka's Inverness Lodge is the perfect way to get back to nature and romance. Stay in any of their lovely rooms or cabins, or perhaps try the unique and dramatic boathouse. Enjoy an exquisite dinner over candlelight in the main lodge. Eat breakfast in bed or in the breakfast nook as you watch a northern harrier through the bird-watching window. Take a walk in the woods. Whatever you decide to do while relaxing at Manka's, you won't be disappointed that you've chosen this rustic woodland getaway.

Sonoma Coast Villa Inn and Spa

16702 Coast Hwy. 1
Bodega, CA 94922
Telephone: 707-876-9818
Reservations: 888-404-2255
www.scvilla.com

Highlights

- Massage and spa services
- Just minutes from the Bodega Harbor Golf Links, Bodega Bay and the Pacific Ocean, and world renowned wineries
- Nine-hole putting green
- Hosting and coordinating for weddings
- In-room amenities: fresh flowers, refrigerator stocked with wine and beverages, fresh ground organic coffee, fruit basket and snacks, wood burning fireplace, and TV/VCR and CD player
- Handicapped accessible
- Rates from $175 to $325

Where is everybody?" is often the first thought that comes to mind as guests turn the ignition off and step out of the car. This kind of quiet is unbelievable and only minutes from the beautiful California coast and the breathtaking hamlet of Bodega Bay. The peaceful and pastoral Sonoma Coast Villa is nestled into 60 acres of private estate pastureland, with sprawling terraced grounds and terracotta stucco walkways connecting 16 Mediterranean-style rooms. It is a rare find.

A ringing phone won't break the spell you're sure to be under at this unusually quiet getaway spot; the suites simply don't have them. Far away from daily distractions, there's plenty to do to help you unwind. Guests can

SONOMA COAST VILLA INN AND SPA EVENING ENTRANCE

take afternoon or moonlight strolls through the courtyard; soak in their own private bath or lovely shared Jacuzzi and pool; unwind with a salt scrub or Swedish full-body massage at the Villa's divine Courtyard Spa; or simply enjoy a glass of wine from one of the area's many local vineyards, either in the privacy of their own room or in the company of other guests during the inn's complimentary wine hour offered each afternoon.

Sonoma Coast Villa, built as a private estate in 1976 by Brian Whetherhill and Bernard Janson, soon became the second site of San Francisco's famous Blue Boar Restaurant. Cyrus and Susan Griffin purchased it in 1992 and lovingly refurbished it, creating the exquisite country inn you'll find today. New owners Ingrid and Johannes Zacabauer are continuiing the fine tradition of gracious hospitality. The area holds another, quirkier claim to fame—it was the film site of Alfred Hitchcock's 1962 classic *The Birds*, something that still draws Hitchcock fans to the area today.

The Villa's front desk concierge service can assist you in planning an adventure-filled day. From a host of activities, you can choose to golf at the 18-hole Bodega Harbour Golf Links; bicycle and hike on numerous nearby trails (bicycles can be rented in Bodega Bay); or kayak, surf, and ride horses at the beach. For the daring, hot air balloon rides are available—a perfect way to see all of beautiful Sonoma County.

During a stay at Sonoma Coast Villa Inn and Spa, you could easily meet a couple who were married there and return each year to celebrate their anniversary. Why? Because once you've experienced the Inn's ambiance and utter tranquility, the urge to return is almost irresistible. And if you have yet to take your vows, but are seriously scouting possible locations, the Villa's Carriage House offers a breathtaking garden setting and patio—perfect for a country wedding and reception—which the Inn's expert staff can help you plan.

In addition to a number of in-room amenities (including fresh organic coffee; a refrigerator stocked with wine and beverages; fruit basket and snacks; a set and ready wood-burning fireplace; CD player, VCR, and satellite TV), the Villa also offers a full country breakfast and afternoon wine hour, as well as a plentiful buffet dinner every Friday and Saturday evening. Room prices vary seasonally, but the charm and serenity are perennial.

Disconnect from the often-hectic modern world and let Ingrid and Johannes, along with the gracious staff at the Sonoma Coast Villa Inn and Spa, pamper you the Old World way.

SONOMA COAST VILLA INN AND SPA RESTAURANT

Fairmont Sonoma Mission Inn & Spa

Sonoma, CA 95476
Telephone: 707-938-9000
Reservations: 800-862-4945
www.fairmont.com

Highlights

♦ Historic spa resort property dating from 1927

♦ Mobil Four-Star and AAA Four-Diamond resort

♦ Grand three-story California mission revival style main building

♦ Pools and spas fed by geothermal mineral springs

♦ Acclaimed 43,000 square-foot European Spa offers full range of services

♦ Complimentary health club and fitness classes

♦ Award-winning Sante restaurant

♦ 45 minutes north of San Francisco

♦ Four handicapped-accessible rooms

♦ Rates from $239 to $1,000

Love at first sight—that's how I felt when I turned off from Highway 12 on the outskirts of Sonoma and drove down the long entry drive. The broad elliptical, manicured lawn blazed with an explosion of flowers. Built in 1927, the matriarch of Northern California resorts was designed in a classic mission revival style, complete with the world's largest (at the time) glass-enclosed swimming pool fed by mineral water from underground springs.

Twin bell towers accent the pink stucco facade, canvas awnings, and Spanish-tile roofing. Inside, the recently restored lobby offers a cozy sense

Fairmont Sonoma Mission Inn & Spa

of welcome, with plush furnishings and original works of art. In addition to a bar, restaurant, and meeting rooms, there are 97 completely refurbished guest quarters in the main building.

For those who want some of the contemporary touches, especially extra space to sprawl and lounge around, the 75 "Wine Country" rooms are highly recommended. Built in 1985, the spacious "new" units are located in freestanding three-story structures that handsomely compliment the main inn. All guestrooms (many with outdoor decks) are outfitted with country-style soft goods, fine prints on the walls, decorator furnishings, and ample use of granite, tile, and marble in the baths.

The Mission Inn signature "Peaches and Cream" soaps, shampoos, and body lotions are highly coveted bath amenities. The soaps and body lotions serve as a fitting prelude to what this place is really all about. You see, it's true that the Mission Inn is highly recommended for rest and relaxation or to do nothing more than enjoy the fine cuisine and lounge around the pool. But, for those who are overdue for some serious indulging, definitely make a date at the Mission Inn's spa. After all, the Fairmont Sonoma Mission Inn is regarded as one of the West Coast's most legendary spas.

Touted as one of California's most comprehensive spa facilities, with a staff in excess of 100 fully trained and licensed practitioners, the services and treatments leave nothing wanting. For example, if you're aching for a massage, the menu includes Swedish-Esalen, aromatherapy, bio-energy, reflexology, sports, and shiatsu. From body wraps to scrubs and back treatments, there's a treatment suited to every sensibility. In addition to more than 40 spa treatments, there are indoor and outdoor spas, a swimming pool, and a lap pool.

The spas and pools are filled with artesian water (containing more than 25 naturally occurring minerals) pumped from 1,100 feet directly below the Inn. The mineral waters are fed into the pools between 86 and 90 degrees.

Ready for more? How about an extensive array of mind/body classes, a tarot card reading, color analysis, the art of illusion dressing, style definition consultations, and guided Wine-Country hikes. I mustn't forget to mention

Fairmont Sonoma Mission & Spa bath

hand and foot care, extensive free weight and exercise equipment, complete hair care services, a steam room, body waxing, aqua aerobics and tennis (including singles and doubles lessons) on championship courts.

All over the world, you'll find menus in fine eateries touting "*Sonoma Valley* Greens, Roast *Sonoma* Duck and Grilled *Sonoma* Lamb." The Mission Inn's "Cafe" and "Grill" restaurants have the envious position of being located mere minutes from the very Sonoma Valley farms and ranches that supply the world's finest eateries. The combination of the freshest organic products with culinary wizardry creates world-class presentations that have received rave reviews from international publications, including *Conde Naste, Forbes,* and a cover feature in *Bon Appétit*. If your itinerary precludes an overnight at the Mission Inn, you can still make a dinner date at the Grill and a massage for two.

Bodega Bay Lodge & Spa

103 Coast Highway One
Bodega Bay, CA 94923
Telephone: 707-875-3525
Reservations: 800-368-2468, ext. 5
www.bodegabaylodge.com

Highlights

- Luxurious guestrooms and suites
- Ocean-view pool, enclosed whirlpool, and full service spa
- Fitness center, sauna
- Beautifully landscaped grounds
- Complimentary Wine Hour daily
- Special romantic getaway packages available
- Stay & Play Golf Package with Bodega Harbour Golf Links
- Handicapped accessible
- Rates from $230 to $465

Leaving behind the hustle and bustle of San Francisco, our drive north along the coast takes us into some of the most beautiful landscapes imaginable. To our left, sea and coastline, on our right, groves of trees punctuated by sweeping hills spotted with grazing cattle. Motoring through this wonderland for an hour, we suddenly come upon a rocky cove with signs of a small town ahead. Just before entering the village of Bodega Bay (population, 950) we turn into the Bodega Bay Lodge and Spa, with its modern yet rustic wood and stone architecture. We are welcomed by the lodge's friendly staff and soon find ourselves settling into the lap of luxury in the Ocean Club suite known as Long-Billed Curlew.

Bodega Bay Lodge & Spa pool

In addition to its 78 beautifully appointed guestrooms, the Bodega Bay Lodge & Spa features five Ocean Club suites. Each suite features an extensive list of in-room amenities to complement the breathtaking view of the surrounding landscape. These suites are named for local birds ("California Quail," "Long-Billed Curlew," "Brown Pelican") and each one offers wide-sweeping views of Doran Beach and Bodega Bay Harbour as well as the opportunity to see the suites' namesake. Each suite features original artwork and lush fabrics. The bedroom area has a king size bed, 27-inch television,

CD-stereo, and desk. An archway leads into the living room area with sofa and recliner; the black granite fireplace surrounded by rich cherry wood shelving intimates an evening of warmth amidst splendid comfort. The luxurious bath includes an oval jet tub with granite surround, separate walk-in ceramic-tiled shower with skylight, large vanity with double sinks, and brass accents.

A stay at the Bodega Bay offers varied opportunities for play and adventure. For those wanting to explore the waterlife by kayak, you can rent single or double kayaks for solo trips or go with guides. You can take your kayak out on the bay or venture up river passages. The area has many miles of trails for horseback riding that take you from the breathtaking vistas of mountain tops, through grassy meadows, and down to coastal dunes and white sand beaches.

Next door to the Bodega Bay Lodge and Spa you'll find the Bodega Harbor Golf Links, designed by Robert Trent Jones, Jr. Mr. Jones designed a true Scottish seaside links course, reminiscent of those found in the birthplace of golf. The course is demanding, yet very playable for the average golfer—as are most of Mr. Jones's courses, depending on which tees you play from. The combination of rolling fairways, deep pot bunkers, undulating greens, native coastal rough, and seaside marshes create a spectacular golf setting.

After a day of play, indulge in the lodge's full-service spa. Spa services include massage, facials, body treatments, and access to the fitness center, pool, and whirlpool. The expert staff will relieve you of any stress not yet dissipated from your sojourn in this place of peace. The spa experience is complemented by hand-delivered terry robes, Italian-made sandals, and a key to the juice bar.

The Bodega Bay Lodge & Spa offers a romantic retreat that is nothing short of sublime—the perfect blend of dramatic coastline, recreation, and elegant hospitality.

Applewood Inn

13555 Highway 116
Guerneville, CA 95446
Telephone: 707-869-9093
Reservations: 800-555-8509
www.applewoodinn.com

Highlights:

♦ Peaceful setting in redwood groves

♦ Upscale accommodations with casual Russian River ambiance

♦ Highly acclaimed restaurant and wine cellar

♦ Original inn is a beautifully preserved 1922 landmark

♦ Nineteen exquisitely decorated rooms

♦ One wheelchair-accessible room

♦ Rates from $185 to $345

Set back from Highway 116 near Guerneville, this stylish inn shares the cozy ambiance of other Russian River resorts while adding an upscale sophistication rarely found in this area. Away from traffic, encircled by towering redwoods and apple orchards, the inn offers a quiet "rustic" experience that includes some of the finest dining around.

Applewood's Mission Revival buildings resemble a Mediterranean villa, with salmon-pink stucco exterior, dark green trim, and pitched, red-tiled roof. The inn is centered around a gravel courtyard with a bubbling fountain.

Belden House, the inn's original 1920s lodge, is a historic landmark with a box-beam ceiling and two living rooms split by a double-sided river-rock fireplace. A lovely dining room with a magnificent crystal chandelier is available for private parties. The guest rooms are cozy and inviting, with private baths, queen-sized beds, TVs, and phones.

APPLEWOOD INN GUEST ROOM

Piccola Casa and Gate House are the inn's newer, more luxurious additions, each a complex of suites with romantic bedside fireplaces and couple showers or whirlpool baths for two.

Throughout the inn, you will find country French furnishings, dark wood molding, unglazed tile floors, featherbeds with hand-pressed linens, and family heirlooms. The color schemes are muted, the lighting soft, the overall effect handsome and understated. Amenities like thick oversize towels, Frette robes, lead crystal drinking glasses, and reading lights on both sides of the bed abound.

Though the flawless marriage of natural beauty and man-made luxury would be reason enough to visit Applewood, many come just for the pleasure of dining here. The restaurant and wine cellar are housed in a French-style barn. At the entrance to the restaurant, there's an elegant, carved copper wine bar and a river-rock fireplace. In the summer, tables are set up on the large adjacent patio.

The executive chef changes the menu daily and takes advantage of the inn's two-acre organic garden. From appetizer to dessert, our meal was outstanding and the service superb.

Even breakfast at Applewood is gourmet quality. We were treated to French toast with candied walnuts and orange Grand Marnier syrup, granola topped with kiwi, applewood-smoked bacon, bruleéd bananas, fresh mango, pineapple, and kiwi, and cranberry or fresh orange juice.

Although summer is "the season" along the Russian River, Applewood is a wonderful place to visit any time of year. When we visited in winter, it seemed magical. We kept warm by the fireplace while we looked out our window at redwoods shrouded in fog. Owners Darryl Notter and Jim Caron told us that when rains come and the river runs high, getting in or out of the inn can be difficult or impossible. Not to worry, we decided. Being stranded at Applewood would suit us just fine.

The Inn at Occidental

PO Box 357
3657 Church Street
Occidental, CA 95465
Telephone: 707-874-1047
Reservations: 800-522-6324
www.innatoccidental.com

Highlights

♦ Located in the heart of a quaint, historic railroad town one hour north of the Golden Gate Bridge

♦ Mobil Four-Star and AAA Four-Diamond location

♦ Extensively remodeled 1870s homestead

♦ Eight rooms and suites all uniquely decorated

♦ Extraordinary dinners and scheduled winemaker evenings

♦ Excellent wedding, honeymoon, and business retreat

♦ Handicapped accessible

♦ Rates from $199 to $329

It is no accident that the Inn at Occidental is one of Northern California's most captivating hideaways. Originally built as a homestead in 1877, the structure later served as the Occidental Water Bottling Company and subsequently transformed into the Heart's Desire Bed & Breakfast. The original owner, Jack Bullard, spent months extensively renovating the Inn. When he opened his doors for business in January 1994, the Inn at Occidental glistened with fine crystal, china, and museum-quality antique furnishings. Now owned by Jerry and Tina Wolsborn, the Inn still has a fine collection of silver, glass, quilts, and antiques toys.

THE INN AT OCCIDENTAL LIVING ROOM

The inn's character and elegant motif are distinctly communicated from afar—the front of the inn features a flower-festooned veranda complete with white wicker chairs and couches. A broad side-yard, highlighted by a large fountain and a profusion of flowerbeds, is frequently used for wedding ceremonies and receptions.

There are eight guest rooms, each of which include amenities such as feather beds, private baths, gas fireplaces, Aveda toiletries, and spa tubs for two. The Inn offers a complete concierge service. Each morning, guests are greeted with complimentary coffee, tea, or cocoa. Breakfast at the Inn iincludes fruit, fresh-baked pastries, pecan waffles, smoked salmon hash, and orange pancakes. Each evening, wine, cheese, and hors d'oeuvres are set out in the lobby.

Though you will have to go out of your way to find the Inn at Occidental, rest assured, once you settle in, this quaint town and the enchanting inn will remain with you as a fond travel memory for years to come.

Heritage House Inn

5200 Highway One
Little River, CA 95456
Telephone: 707-937-5885
Reservations: 800-235-5885
www.heritagehouseinn.com

Highlights

◆ Historic main house built in 1877

◆ Antique schoolhouse, firehouse, barbershop, and water tower serve as romantic guest accommodations

◆ 37-acres, 66 units, many with fireplaces or stoves, private and semi-private decks, and private baths

◆ Excellent whale-watching location

◆ On-site gift shop

◆ Fully handicapped-accessible/equipped room

◆ Rates from $125 to $425

Heritage House is among the largest inns on the North Coast, yet you would never know it as the oceanfront inn encompasses 37-acres of lush native vegetation, cypress, and fir trees.

Many people who stay at the cliffside retreat immediately experience an uncanny sense of déja vu. Before long the mystery is usually solved when they learn that the property was utilized as the film location for *Same Time, Next Year*, starring Allan Alda and Ellen Burstyn. As an interesting aside, the author wrote the hit play and subsequent movie script while staying in one of the cottages. We weren't surprised when the innkeeper told us that the two "Same Time, Next Year" accommodations are among the most frequently requested.

THE MENDOCINO COAST

The absence of in-room TV's and telephones creates withdrawal symptoms for some, but once most people settle in and let go of their urban baggage they discover that the lack of technological amenities is an essential ingredient in the Heritage House experience. Blessed with a spectacular oceanfront location and easily navigated pathways down to the seashore, this award-winning destination is superb for whale watching.

Most of the accommodations are located in cottage-style structures. A majority of the rooms and suites have ocean views, antique furnishings, wood burning fireplaces or stoves, large private or semi-private decks, wet bars, and Jacuzzi tubs.

When it comes time to dine, you're in for a real culinary treat, as Heritage House has long been known for its outstanding cuisine. *Gault Millau,* a top European-based guide book, in concert with a flotilla of other prestigious international and regional travel publications, repeatedly rank Heritage House Restaurant and Inn among the best in the West.

The original 1877 farmhouse has been extensively remodeled and expanded over the years and presently contains the main dining room, reception area, cocktail lounge, three guest rooms, and library with leather-bound books and historic photos.

You've come to the right place if you are a wine enthusiast, as the wine list is repeatedly ranked among the top 200 in the world by *Wine Spectator Magazine.* If you plan to arrive in March, be sure to inquire about the annual Heritage Wine Series that includes wine-maker dinners and tastings hosted by top regional vintners. All three dining rooms, including the Applehouse Lounge are situated to maximize the spectacular vistas. The main dining room has a majestic domed ceiling.

The Heritage House has been a part of the North Coast travel experience since 1949 and is presently owned and operated by a local family. The property was historically known as Pullen's Landing when the waterfront was utilized for transferring redwood timber to waiting schooners that shipped the lumber to the Gold Rush boom-town of San Francisco. During the latter 19th Century, the farmhouse was used as a safe house for Chinese laborers smuggled into the country to work the mines, forests, and railroads.

The homestead was eventually abandoned, but during prohibition Baby Face Nelson hid out in the then boarded-up farmhouse and used the adjacent beach for his bootleg operations. At least Baby Face had one redeeming characteristic—the good taste to choose a stunningly beautiful hideout.

The Stanford Inn by the Sea

Coast Highway & Comptche Ukiah Rd.
Mendocino, CA 95460
Telephone: 707-937-5615
Reservations: 800-331-8884
www.stanfordinn.com

Highlights

- Awesome vistas of the Pacific and the village of Mendocino

- AAA Four-Diamond award-winning inn

- Ten-acre property is adjacent to the Big River and just a short stroll to the seashore and town

- Nine suites, 32 richly appointed rooms, all with country-style antiques, four-poster or sleigh beds, fireplaces, and TV/VCR/CD units

- Greenhouse-enclosed swimming pool, exercise room with Universal equipment, sauna, and Jacuzzi

- Pets welcomed

- Mountain bikes, canoes, and kayaks available on-site

- Exceptional full breakfast with vegan options. Garden-driven breakfast includes eggs portabella and The Ravens garden polenta

- Massage in-room or on-site at the Inn's Massage in the Forest

- Rates from $256 to $295 and suites from $345 to $465

Upon entering our room we were instantaneously spellbound by the dazzling panorama framed by the wide open French doors. In the middle foreground, a gently rolling meadow was loaded with ample images to handsomely fill a painter's canvas—llamas lazily munched on hay, while two swans languidly floated on an adjacent pond.

STANFORD INN BY THE SEA BISHOP ROOM

Fir and fruit trees and rows of raised planting beds brimming with herbs and flowers punctuated the thick-green grassy field that flawlessly accented the rugged cliff-edge and the seething blue Pacific beyond.

Off to the right, the land dropped sharply and terminated at the edge of Big River. The village of Mendocino, a quarter-mile off, was neatly framed by an orchestrated break in a row of towering fir trees. The scene was amplified by the dreamy nineteenth-century white-painted Presbyterian Church steeple towering above the surrounding businesses and Victorian-era homes.

This is the point in a resort-destination story when my inner editor-voice starts nagging, "Get to the point, stupid—tell them about the firmness of the bed, the plushness of the comforters, the in-room coffee maker, the fresh flowers in the room, the excellent bottle of wine awaiting you on the silver platter and the sumptuous breakfast cooked to order." Well, those are indeed essential qualities for a first-class property, but the more places I visit the more I realize that the essential elements are often intangible and border on things spiritual. It is frequently the setting, the surrounding environment and especially the human element that make for superlative experiences and passionate memories.

Much of the credit at Stanford Inn goes to innkeepers, Joan and Jeff Stanford, who have propelled and nurtured what nature started. When the Stanfords purchased the property in 1980, they resolutely set out to make their little slice of heaven decidedly outstanding.

Guests are provided with an ultra-romantic setting and top-quality amenities and services. But one facet of the Stanford's mission isn't readily apparent—their firm commitment to conduct their business in an environmentally responsible manner. All metal, glass, and paper products are sorted and recycled at the Inn. The Stanfords on-site Big River Nursery (a California-certified organic farm) provides dried flowers and wreaths, herbs, vegetables, lettuce, and other produce to their acclaimed restaurant, The Ravens.

The Stanfords' full-circle approach to things organic is symbolic of how they deal with their staff and the activities offered by the inn. The Stanfords seek out the best local people for a given job, empower and treat their employees with respect, and pay them more than the requisite "going rate." Consequently the Stanfords speak with pride of their employees' longevity and their friendly, compassionate attitudes.

After a day of exploring the village, biking, hiking, and canoeing, the Stanfords offer the perfect place to relax and soothe those sore muscles: a massive greenhouse structure that houses a large heated pool, as well as a Jacuzzi and sauna. The greenhouse pool area is embellished with giant fishtail palms, orchids, and other tropical treasures that make this lush environment truly fanciful.

From the engaging rooms and cuisine to the romantic atmosphere and awesome surrounding vistas, the Stanford Inn is the perfect getaway spot. With all the essential amenities of a first-class inn, as well as that special air of things sublime, the Stanford Inn is in a coveted league of its own.

Glendeven Inn

8205 North Highway 1
Little River, CA 95456
Telephone: 707-937-0083
Reservations: 800-822-4536
www.glendeven.com

Highlights

- Nestled between the coastal forest and the ocean on ten rural acres

- High-quality art displayed throughout the inn and in Partners Gallery

- Meticulously maintained, spacious guest rooms, most with ocean views, porches or decks, and wood-burning fireplaces

- Across a meadow from the inn is a two-bedroom, two-bath vacation house with a hot tub, full kitchen, beautiful gardens, and fantastic ocean views

- Two miles from Mendocino, and a short walk through surrounding Van Damme State Park to the ocean

- Historical legacy of an 1860s Federalist-style farmhouse, with barn and water tower

- Complimentary full breakfast delivered to the room, wine and hors d'oeuvres in the evenings, and homemade cookies and hot beverages available 24 hours

- One wheelchair-accessible room (wheelchair fits in room but not shower)

- Rates for 10 rooms in the inn $130 to $275; vacation house rates from $255 to $410

THE GLENDEVEN INN

One of the most appealing places to stay in Mendocino is actually two miles south in Little River, just above the entrance to Van Damme State Park. Situated in a park-like setting across from the ocean, Glendeven Inn perfectly blends simple country pleasures with elegant comfort and gracious service. But the piece d'resistance is the well-chosen art displayed throughout the inn and in a contemporary art gallery operated by a partnership of ten local artists who feature new shows every month.

The heart of Glendeven is a beautifully restored New England-style Federalist farmhouse surrounded by forests, meadows, and acres of ever-flowering gardens. Guest quarters in the Farmhouse, Stevenscroft annex, and private Carriage House Suite provide undisturbed luxury, combining tasteful antiques, comfortable furniture, and fine art. All accommodations feature well-lighted reading areas and private bathrooms. Most have fireplaces, private decks, and views of the ocean.

Delicious hot country breakfasts are brought to your room to begin the day, and informal early evening gatherings in the Farmhouse living room with wine and hors d'oeuvres prepare you for Mendocino's extraordinary dining experiences.

Bay View, an upstairs room in the Farmhouse with a fireplace, sitting area, and deck offers a calming view of the inn's gardens, surrounding meadow, and the ocean just beyond. In keeping with the inn's emphasis on quiet solitude, there is no phone or TV. A CD player and a collection of classical CD's are thoughtfully provided, however. Tucked away in downy comfort, most guests will sleep soundly, but the traffic from Highway 1 could bother light sleepers who might want to sleep in rooms set further back from the road.

The Garden Room, downstairs next to the reception area, is the inn's least expensive room. Although it has no ocean view and is smaller than the other rooms, it's a favorite simply because of its cheerful, garden-like decor. For those who love a long soak in the tub, note that it's also the only room in the inn with a bathtub. Most guest rooms have tiled showers only.

At the very top of Farmhouse, tucked under the eaves, is the Garret, a cozy and romantic, dormer-windowed room with the best views of the ocean available at Glendeven.

Located in the Stevenscroft annex, the Bay Loft room—with its soft muted tones, redwood detailing, cozy bed alcove and skylights—is yet another favorite among guests. Like the other rooms, it also has a fireplace and a separate sitting area.

The Carriage House Suite is the epitome of luxurious seclusion, located all by itself on the second floor above the art gallery. It has a marvelous sitting room with fireplace, several comfortable reading areas, refrigerator, coffeemaker, and microwave. The bedroom has another fireplace near the brass king-size sleigh bed, and the beautiful bathroom features a two-person shower and bidet. Breakfast on the Carriage House's balcony overlooking private gardens is a fine way to start the day.

For families or friends traveling together, Glendeven's vacation house, La Bella Vista, offers plenty of space—two bedrooms and two full baths, living room with TV, library, fully-outfitted kitchen, lots of decks, a hot tub, and colorful gardens. Children are welcome, but a maximum of four people is allowed.

On some foggy Mendocino mornings, visitors often choose to enjoy breakfast in front of the fire, but on sunny, clear days they might instead consider eating on the balcony with the hope of spotting a deer or two. But even if the deer aren't cooperating, certainly everything else about your visit to Glendeven will likely be divine.

Joshua Grindle Inn

44800 Little Lake Road
Mendocino, CA 95460
Telephone: 707-937-4143
Reservations: 1-800-GRINDLE
www.joshgrin.com

Highlights

♦ 1879 Victorian built by Joshua Grindle, the town banker

♦ Enchanting vistas of the village and the sea beyond

♦ Convenient location within easy stroll of all Mendocino attractions

♦ Five rooms and suites in Main House, detached Saltbox Cottage with two rooms, and three romantic Water Tower accommodations

♦ Impeccably appointed interior decor and period furnishings

♦ Excellent gourmet breakfast

♦ No handicapped-accessible accommodations

♦ Rates from $179 to $375; off-season rates midweek November through June

The ageless, watercolor-white picket fence out front sets the tone and serves as the perfect accent for this New England-style home that has been a beguiling part of Mendocino's townscape since 1879.

The Joshua Grindle's interior is masterfully outfitted with Early American antiques and unusual, original prints and artworks. The main parlor, highlighted by an ancient but pristine pump organ and a vintage fireplace, is so deftly furnished that you'll feel as if you are a special guest in a private residence. Afternoon sherry served in the parlor and evening platters of cookies are but a few of the special touches at Joshua Grindle.

In the morning, a full gourmet breakfast is served in the dining room. Here guests share their adventures and discoveries while sitting around a

Joshua Grindle Inn

circa-1830s pine harvest table and munching on home made dishes that include muffins, scones, frittatas, quiches, an abundance of fresh fruits, cereals, yogurt, coffees, and teas.

All of the guest rooms have their own special charms, but given the opportunity, our first choice would be to book a room in the water tower—if for no other reason than a stay in a water tower just sounds so romantic.

Watertower I is located on the ground level with a redwood beam ceiling and Early American pine furnishings. There is a sitting area with a Vermont Casting fireplace, queen bed, and a deep soak tub/shower. This room is also surrounded by private gardens, offering the guest the sense of being in their own little world.

Upstairs in Watertower II, you have the sense of being in a tree house. Through gaps in the encapsulating Cypress trees there's a peak at the sometimes seething and sometimes-placid Pacific Ocean. There's also a fireplace, queen bed, sitting area, and private bath with a deep-soak tub/shower.

Close by is the Saltbox Cottage with two rooms, both with Franklin fireplaces, queen beds, private baths with tub/showers and open beam cedar ceilings.

Each of the five rooms in the Victorian House offer something different. Nautical is appropriately outfitted with blues and whites and nautical touches throughout. This enticing room, with a queen bed and private bath with tub/shower, is ideal for those who enjoy a lazy late afternoon or early morning in-room lounge-fest on a daybed next to a multi-pane wood window with excellent overlooks of the village and a peak at the ocean.

Grindle is appropriately the room where old Josh slept. There's a sitting area with views of town and the ocean, a four poster queen bed, and private bath with shower only. Library is appropriately furnished with floor-to-ceiling bookshelves, a four poster queen bed, a fireplace, and private bath with a deep soaking tub/shower. Treeview offers enchanting vistas of the adjacent cypress trees and the watertower. With floral wallpaper and accents, there's a sitting area, queen bed, and deep soaking tub/shower in the private bath. Master is light and airy with views of the apple trees and gardens out back, a brick courtyard, a sitting area adjacent to a fireplace and a luxurious bathroom with a whirlpool tub and separate shower.

The Joshua Grindle evokes such an enchanting sense of home that we couldn't resist the urge to delay the commencement of our morning explorations. We stepped out the front door headed for the car, but found ourselves seduced by the Adirondack chairs on the front verandah. So there we sat, sucking up the scent of salt air accented with the hint of pine smoke from a nearby chimney, quite content to do absolutely nothing except savor the moment—a glorious morning in Mendocino.

Joshua Grindle Inn
window view

The Gingerbread Mansion

400 Berding Street
Ferndale, CA 95536
Telephone: 707-786-4000
Reservations: 800-952-4136
www.gingerbread-mansion.com

Highlights

- Intricately detailed, 1899 combination Queen Ann and Eastlake Victorian is a true "painted lady"

- Mobil Four-Star and AAA Four-Diamond resort

- 11 rooms and suites with private baths, and romantic elements such as fireplaces, his-and-hers claw foot tubs, and garden views

- Formal English-style garden is a special treat and makes an ideal wedding site

- Continental breakfast served in the dining room or in the privacy of your room

- Use of cruiser bicycles for exploring the Victorian village of Ferndale

- Rates from $160 to $400; inquire about winter specials

The entire village of Ferndale is officially recognized by the State of California as a Historic Landmark and the Main Street District is a registered National Historic Landmark. Much of the town is comprised of Victorian-era homes, business buildings and churches, and the Gingerbread Mansion has earned its place as Ferndale's ambassador to the world.

The house was built in 1899 for Ferndale physician, Dr. Hogan J. Ring, who converted his home into a hospital in 1920. Unfortunately, Hogan's Ferndale Hospital went bankrupt within three years and it subsequently served as a rest home.

THE GINGERBREAD MANSION FRONT FACADE

In 1981 Ken Torbert was sightseeing in the town of Ferndale when he happened upon the ornately garnished Victorian and noticed a for sale sign in the front yard. Days later, Torbert signed papers and became the proud owner of a monstrous 10,000 square foot home in dire need of major renovation.

The inn opened for business in 1983 and today the Gingerbread Mansion is a showcase of Torbert's extraordinary talents as an interior designer and innkeeper par excellence. The exterior, signature peach and yellow tone colors and all of the interior finishes such as the rich wallpaper patterns, soft goods and exquisite antique furnishings were hand picked and orchestrated by Torbert, who recently sold the inn to Robert and Julie McInroy and Sue and Vince Arriaga.

Each of the nine rooms and suites are distinctly different from one another but they are all equally pleasing and inviting. For example, step into the Gingerbread Suite and you will probably smile as you spot the two claw foot bathtubs, and fireplace—right in bedroom. Down the hall, the Fountain Suite's bathroom is graced with two side-by-side claw foot tubs.

The Empire Suite is accessed via a private entry with Victorian stained glass French doors, large bathing area with a marble and glass shower, and over-sized porcelain tub in front of a fireplace. A full living and dining area complete the opposite side of the suite with a second fireplace.

The Hideaway Room is an inviting abode with a dramatic stained glass window gracing the exterior steep-pitched gable-end wall. An enticing sleeping loft with a single bed makes a tempting reading and lounging hideout, while down below, the smartly decorated room has a queen bed and bath.

If you have a fondness for formal gardens, then by all means request the Garden Room. In the evening the fireplace warms this mirthful space, while in the morning, you'll be tempted to throw open the French doors overlooking the gardens and request breakfast in bed.

Strawberry Hill Room, distinguished with ample windows, is a bright and cheerful zone of privacy with a tub shower combination in the bath and a dressing area.

Zipporah's Room is small but offers a sense of intimacy and also has excellent vistas of the mountains surrounding Ferndale.

Not surprisingly, the Lilac Room is fittingly accented with lilac accents and touches. This spacious room has a claw foot tub and scintillating views of the gardens.

Make a date for a rendezvous in the Heron Suite and you'll definitely feel as if you were in an authentic Victorian-era bedroom suite. Originally two rooms, Heron offers a spacious bathroom, an antique writing desk, sitting area and ample space to spread out, with the added bonus of great town and country views through the double hung wood windows.

Carter House, Hotel Carter, and Restaurant 301

301 L Street
Eureka, CA 95501
Telephone: 707-440-8062
Reservations: 800-404-1390
www.carterhouse.com

Highlights

- Original Carter House, Bell Cottage, Carter Cottage, and Hotel Carter

- Exemplary, friendly staff, concierge service, dry cleaning, and other special four-star amenities

- Restaurant 301's exquisite cuisine among the best in all of northern California

- Complimentary breakfast

- Regularly scheduled wine-maker dinners featuring some of the state's top vintners

- Rooms and suites outfitted with custom antique pine furnishings, fireplaces, and VCR/CD/TV units (some even have whirlpool tubs)

- Extensive in-house video and CD library

- Evening wine and hors d'oeuvres and bedtime herbal tea service with fresh baked cookies

- One handicapped-accessible room

- Rates from $185 to $595 (including full breakfast, wine, and hors d'oeuvres)

Pure and simple—this is a place of sublime serenity and class. All credit begins with Mark and Christi Carter, two of the most gracious and charismatic innkeepers in the country, but ultimately, the success of the enterprise is due to their gracious and attentive staff.

The dynamic duo didn't start out with a vision of operating one of the top-rated inns in the United States. All they wanted to do was build a meticulously crafted, accurate recreation of a 1906 San Francisco Victorian for their personal residence.

Eventually they struck on the idea of opening up a portion of their abode as a bed and breakfast. They did, and the guests came in droves. Their B&B quickly became the rage with vacationers from around the state and world.

If your sensibilities tend toward the intimacy of a small inn or B&B, then the Carter House is for you. But be forewarned, the Carter House interior decor is whimsical, light, and airy—without the layered, frilly trappings frequently associated with B&Bs.

CARTER HOUSE RESTAURANT 301

The Carters' interior design statement is minimalist. There isn't an overabundance of furnishings or paintings, but what there is sets an evocative tone of elegance, from the original paintings and prints to the antique furnishings. The five rooms create a homey environment, albeit a very grand and spacious one, complete with massive crown molding, dark wainscoting, and solid oak panel doors.

Restaurant 301 and the 23-room Carter Hotel are located diagonally across the street from Carter House and are modeled after a long-vanished Victorian-era hostelry. The hotel has become a handsome companion to the Carters' original inn, as well as a gentrified Eureka landmark and one of the city's most popular dining spots.

The Hotel Carter embodies the same qualities as the Carter House, with the added ambiance of an intimate European-style hotel. The dining room and main lobby area of the hotel are bathed with natural light from multi-pane windows that reach toward the high ceiling. The outstanding original artwork and pastel colored walls infuse this public space with a captivating sense of warmth and welcome. The sitting area adjacent to the lobby fireplace is a favorite evening gathering spot where guests chat over wine and hors d'oeuvres.

A lovingly restored Victorian, the Bell Cottage, named after the original owners, was the next addition to the Carter Empire on "L" Street. Situated two doors down from the Carter House, the Bell House offers equally pleasing characteristics and amenities.

The latest addition to the Carter enclave is a lovingly restored Victorian cottage that sits between the Original Carter House and the Bell Cottage. Dubbed "The Carter Cottage," this posh restoration offers the pinnacle of Carter hospitality. With two fireplaces, a lovely commercial kitchen and dining area, two bathrooms, and a marvelous private deck overlooking Humboldt Bay, the Carter Cottage is the perfect setting for romance, relaxation, and culinary enjoyment. Restaurant 301's chef is available to cook a private dinner for Carter Cottage guests, and, of course, the treasure-packed Carter wine cellars are also at the guests' disposal.

The Carters' tenacious demand for perfection and refusal to compromise leaves no room at the inn for things mediocre, and that definitely applies to the food and wine served at Restaurant 301. Mark and Christi share a love of distinguished cuisine. Christi's expertise in envisioning and creating savory dishes and Mark's passion for fine wines makes for a perfect marriage of delectable gourmet offerings complimented by one of the most extensive wine lists and wine cellars on the West Coast. In fact, the Carters' wine list has received a grand award from *Wine Spectator* every year since 1998—placing it among the top 81 dining establishments in the world.

To give you a glimpse of their commitment to things sublime, the Carters' belief in using the freshest ingredients possible spurred them to plant and maintain a prodigious garden (regarded as the largest herb garden serving an inn on the West Coast) boasting more than 300 varieties of vegetables, greens, herbs, fruits, and edible flowers. The Carters encourage their guests to join the chefs in their daily foray to harvest the evening's produce.

Capitalizing on Eureka's seaport location, the Carters purchase the freshest seafood available, and naturally, their menu reflects a masterful melding of fresh greens and fish. A menu sampler includes an appetizer of Humboldt Bay oysters baked with garlic and lemon and topped with Asiago cheese and fennel.

The litmus test of an inn or hotel experience isn't really predicated on the plushness of the carpeting or down comforters; the ultimate factor that determines whether you'll return and recommend the place is usually embodied in the human element. How are you treated by the staff? Do they exhibit a friendly, helpful, and cheerful attitude? Those are critical factors, and I'm pleased to report that the employees here earned an A+.

Once you've experienced the panoply of splendid experiences offered at the Carters' hostelry, you might find yourself smiling the next time you say the word "eureka." After all, it means, "I have found it!"

About the Author

Author and travel writer Thomas Wilmer started his journalism career as a copy boy for the West Coast edition of the *Wall Street Journal* while attending college in the San Francisco Bay area. He's logged over a million miles in his travels across the globe, from Morocco to China, up to the Arctic Circle and down to South Africa. Although Wilmer's writing niche is upscale international travel, his home base in Morro Bay, California, has allowed him ample opportunity to explore the California coast for the past 20 years. Wilmer's writings on California coastal destinations have appeared in numerous magazines, including *Tahoe Quarterly, Arizona Foothills, New Times, Las Vegas Magazine,* and London-based *Prestige Magazine.* He is presently the travel editor at *Central Coast Magazine* in California. His newspaper travel features have appeared in more than 30 North American cities, including Toronto, Phoenix, Salt Lake City, Savannah, Duluth, St. Paul, Pittsburgh, Providence, Charleston, Annapolis, Corpus Christi, and Tampa. His radio travel show, Audiolog, has aired over NPR affiliate stations KCBX and KSBX for more than a decade. Tom is also a licensed general contractor and spent five years as vice president of construction activities with a California-based architectural firm.

Travel Notes